The Anatomy of a
Pummeled Life

Peter M. Talty

Contents

Introduction

When it comes to my youngest brother, Patrick or Pat, I was not my brother's keeper. Instead, unbeknownst to me, I was apparently making his difficult life even more so. However, I choose to use ignorance with a sprinkling of stupidity as my defense.

Until a few months ago, I was either ignorant or unappreciative of the serious burdens my brother Pat carried throughout his challenging life. Because of my chronically ignorant state, I did not realize that the kidding and teasing I did of Pat throughout his life was a form of maltreatment in the form of pummeling. To be clear, let me share the view of pummeling I will use that is drawn from these four interrelated definitions:

- *To beat or thrash with or <u>as if</u> with the fists.*
- *The action of striking repeatedly with or <u>as if</u> with fists.*
- *To attack or harry (torment) verbally.*
- *Criticism or condemnation.*
    (Collins' English Dictionary, 2014)

I underlined the words "as if" in the first two bullets above because it is these two words that are so significant in pummeling. Obviously, one does not need to be physically punched or slapped in order to suffer psychological harm and pain. Other things that can result from pummeling can be feelings of inadequacy, embarrassment, sadness, discouragement, weakness, or defeat. I am sure Pat experienced all these, thanks to me and others.

So, rather than being my brother's keeper, I instead became his pummeler extraordinaire. Why? Because I enjoyed the reactions and praise from my four brothers, and even our mom, whenever I would engage Pat in a conversation that got him to recall how he

1

had made one of his many colossal mistakes in life. His explanations were always unusual and very humorous because of his side comments, providing me with plenty of fodder for my pummelings.

Again, my pummelings of Pat were never physical. However, I did assault him with my words throughout his life. Why? I thought it was all good fun, and I never thought I was hurting him. Of course, I was very wrong, but I did not realize this until it was too late. He died before I saw what I had inadvertently done to him throughout his ill-fated life.

My distorted reasoning before I did the research for this book was that my pummeling of Pat was just me kidding and teasing him. Harming him in any way never entered my mind. Dumb, I know. My brothers and I would kid and tease each other all the time. However, it was different with Pat because Pat was different. He was spoiled, demanding, jealous, humorous, moody, resentful, vindictive, cunning, and manipulative. I think part of the reinforcement for my pummeling came from Pat himself. He would laugh uproariously along with the rest of us. There was often great praise for my wit, timing, creativity, and the ability to always make Pat look foolish, which he was not.

Reflecting on these pummeling encounters, I see that I ignored a different kind of feedback from others who were present. This was from the more sensitive people present, usually female, who did not laugh. Instead, they often said, "Poor Pat." Why did it take 60+ years for me to recognize what was really being said? I don't know, but I do know that these women saw what I could not.

What I did not realize until recently was that I was wounding and diminishing Pat deeply, and unbeknownst to me, he was becoming increasingly and deservedly enraged with me. I did not realize that his distancing himself from me and his silence when we were together were my payback for too much pummeling. Out of

2

ignorance, I continued my merry pummeling ways for many, many years, for which I am now very remorseful.

So, what did I discover in my research about Pat that caused me to change my view of my pummeling of him? It was my discovery that throughout most of his life, Pat carried three major burdens, two of which I did not even realize he was carrying until just a few months ago:

> His first major burden was a chronic health condition that I was aware of because I was there in 1957 when it first happened. I witnessed his first grand mal seizure that terrified us all and led to a lifetime of epilepsy that, despite the diligence of a very caring and skilled neurologist, could not be cured. Neither extensive neurosurgery nor the latest medications and their adjustments could prevent Pat from having spontaneous seizures without warning. This all started when he was just ten years old. The price he paid was the loss of too many jobs, being prevented from getting his driver's license for most of his life, and his inability to forge strong relationships.

> The second burden I discovered when I examined Pat's educational record. He had a severe learning disability that was never diagnosed or treated. Despite being a good problem solver and having a high level of functional intelligence, he just could not find success in the classroom. This resulted in his failing two grades in grammar school and his leaving high school after just six weeks.

> I accidentally came upon Pat's third burden in applying some remarkable research findings that showed how adversities in Pat's early childhood impacted his physical and mental dysfunctions and failures as an adult. I am referring to the six Adverse Childhood Experiences (ACEs) that befell Pat before he reached the age of 19. These ACEs

did not auger well for his future, as will be explained below and in subsequent chapters. Together, these six ACEs were Pat's third burden.

I did not need to do any research to know that Pat was raised in a poor family consumed with toxic stress because I lived alongside him in those many toxic stress-filled home environments. I was four years older and was subsequently trained as an occupational therapist, and it is from these dual perspectives that I had this epiphany: the many misfortunes Pat encountered in life were not of his doing. Because of the three burdens he carried, he was not the author nor navigator of his own life.

The combination or interplay of his three major burdens (epilepsy, learning disability, and high ACEs score) prevented Pat from moving forward and enjoying life. It was not a lack of intelligence or motivation. He was bright and worked hard, but the cumulative impact of his three burdens denied him from being successful in almost every endeavor.

I view these three major burdens as being analogous to anchors that fix a ship in place in a storm. Pat's life, in many ways, was fixed in place. The synergistic combination of his three burdens or anchors was what frequently halted or ambushed him, brought him to his knees, and probably contributed to his premature death. There were times when I tried to help him, but I did not know or appreciate the triple load he was carrying.

Add to his burdens all the incessant pummeling he received at home, in the neighborhood, in school, the Boy Scouts, the workplace, and so on, and you must wonder how he ever rose again. But he did rise repeatedly until he could rise no more.

His tragic life story needs to be told, not because he was pummeled and therefore should be pitied, but because despite his bearing the load of three major burdens and those pummelings, he did rise to fight again and again. I never appreciated how each rising made him less resilient because until recently, I only knew of one of his burdens, his unresolved seizure disorder or epilepsy.

I am the only sibling of Pat's who survives to tell his story. I am one of six. Our parents, siblings, grandparents, aunts, uncles, and all but two cousins are gone. I am it to tell his story, but I do so with help from Pat's biggest protector and advocate: our mother or Ma. Fortunately, she was an avid letter writer and wrote frequently of Pat's struggles and successes. Through her letters over many years, I have her vivid descriptions of what Pat's life was like as he struggled against obstacles carrying his known and unknown burdens. Oddly, she never mentions any pummelings. Does this mean my guilt and shame are less? Sadly, no.

From the time Pat was born on September 22, 1946, until Ma's passing on August 3, 1970, when Pat was 24 years old, she wrote of Pat's hopes, dreams, efforts, disappointments, losses, successes, and failures. Her voice related to Pat will be heard throughout much of this book.

Why me? It is not just because I am here, but I also have other "qualifications." First off, I lived with Pat until I was 24 years-old and directly observed both the numerous pummelings he received from me and others and their aftereffects. I had a great vantage point for many of the pummelings because, in many cases, I was the main pummeler. Despicable!

Pat and I grew up in a close but distressed and impoverished family. Being four years older than Pat, I evolved into different roles related to his needs. At different times, I was Pat's protector, reluctant rescuer, pummeler, advisor, wrestling opponent, and drinking and drugging buddy. His was a complex life full of so many tragedies that I have wanted to write about Pat for a very long time. Now, I must tell it in order to give us both some peace.

Reference

Collins' English Dictionary, 12 ed. (October 23, 2014) Glasgow, Scotland

Chapter 1

Our Family Ruptures!

It is reasonable to assume that most physical and organic structures can only take so much internal or external pressure or stress before they burst or rupture. Rupture is exactly what happened to our family on New Year's Eve in 1954. This catastrophe was the result of what is now known as Toxic Stress rather than the better-known kinds of stress that all families usually experience.

Specifically, Toxic stress is the body's response to lasting and serious stress without enough support from a caregiver. When a child doesn't get the help he needs, his body can't turn off the stress response normally. This long-lasting form of stress can harm a child's body and brain and can cause lifelong physical and mental health problems. Researchers found that toxic stress is prolonged activation of the stress response systems in the absence of protective relationships (Shonkoff, J.P. *Pediatrics*, 2013). If you ever encountered a difficult work situation where you have a lot of responsibility, but no control and your boss refuses to get involved, you would be experiencing toxic stress. However, remember that your adult brain is fully developed and usually hardened to this type of damage, and by the time you encountered toxic stress situations, you probably had developed protective factors. This was not the case for us kids leading up to that fateful New Year's Eve.

To further differentiate regular stress from toxic stress, consider these differences:

Positive Stress is brief increases in heart rate and mild elevations in stress hormone levels.

You experience this kind of positive stress whenever you "psych yourself up" to take on a challenging task.

Tolerable Stress is a serious, temporary stress response buffered by supportive, stable family relationships. Good coaches, loving and patient parents, mentors, the clergy, therapists, and teachers do this all the time.

In 1954, when Pat was 8 years old and I was 12, the strife and toxic stress that my Dad caused in our home, in addition to ongoing poverty, reached the breaking point. Ma and my sister Sue decided to do something about it. So, they conceived and executed a courageous plan of escape on New Year's Eve. I never knew why New Year's Eve was chosen. The plan called for Ma and my younger brothers Danny and Pat to live on an Air Force base in San Antonio, Texas. They would live with my oldest brother, Tommy and his wife, Karoline. My older brother Bernie and I would move in with Sue and her husband Jim and their daughter Kathleen.

Getting Ma, Danny, and Pat to Texas would be achieved using my Dad's railroad pass that would get them as far as St. Louis. Tommy was then going to wire Ma the money to get them the rest of the way to San Antonio using money he hoped to borrow from his corner grocer, who he hardly knew.

Pat, unlike the rest of us, was ecstatic about going on a train and made everybody anxious with his constant chatter and questions. I just remember, for some reason, that I was worrying a lot about Dad. What would he think when he came home to find us all gone? Sue and Ma were adamant about us not leaving him a note about where we all went. I worried that the shock would kill him, but I kept all this to myself.

I was, however, excited to be going to live with Sue and Jim because they were always doing fun things with us, took us places, and they were really our heroes. They had a lot of patience and were always a big help to Ma and very good to us kids.

As far as I was concerned, this was all just so sudden and traumatic. I wondered, would I ever see Ma, Danny, or Pat again? What about all our stuff in the flat? Our furniture was like our clothes: old and ratty. Probably no one would want our stuff. That was so sad. We also didn't get much for Christmas, and what we did get was so cheaply made that most of it fell apart when we tried to use them. The hockey sticks Danny and I got were shattered in the first game we played on Christmas Day. I felt so bad for Ma, who did her best to get us some of the things we wanted, but the money Dad gave her was so little that buying anything of quality was not to be. We had a sad Christmas, and soon, this would be followed by an even sadder New Year's Eve. I knew I was going to miss Danny and Pat and especially Ma. I walked around our destitute flat, trying not to cry without much success.

Yes, we were poor, but at least we were all together. However, in a few hours, that would all change. Ma always carried herself as if we were not poor. Whenever kids made fun of our clothes or the things we didn't have, and that brought us home crying or depressed, Ma, in her stoic voice, would tell us something like this: "You turn right around and go back out there and tell them, 'that your father has a better job than their father ever thought of having'." Initially, we believed it and did what she said. That was until the kids laughed at us and rudely responded with cruel questions like: "Oh yeah? Then how come you don't have a car? Why doesn't your mom have any teeth?" We had no answers, and we stopped crying to Ma, swallowed our tears, and tried to block out the questions we couldn't answer.

The fact was that my dad really did have a really good job. He was very well paid as an engineer on a local railroad. However, we lived a life of poverty because he spent most of his money drinking, gambling, carousing, and philandering. He would be gone for three or four days and nights a week, but I didn't know where he went until my sister explained it to me. That's when I learned what "philandering and carousing" meant.

Regardless, his uncontrolled spending made us poor and greatly in debt to the two local grocery stores and two loan companies, besides a bunch of other unpaid utility and other bills. Ma and Sue went down to the Welfare department and to Catholic Charities for help, but once they learned of Dad's significant salary, Ma was denied. So, our Dad was a "deadbeat dad" before the phrase was even coined. Regardless, Dad was one, and we all suffered because of his wayward ways.

Dad's drinking and spending made us kids poor, scared, resentful of what others had, and ashamed. We were the only family in our working-class neighborhood that had a deadbeat dad and essentially lived a life of poverty. This was the driving source of the toxic stress in our home that impacted all of us kids growing up.

I thought about the great tension I always felt as I walked around our flat for the last time and wondered why our family had to be split up and ruptured. Was there no other way? Apparently not.

Of course, I did not know the damage toxic stress was doing to our brains and bodies as kids until recently, nor did I know how toxic stress was laying the foundation for problems and illnesses in all our futures.

I guess the thinking of Ma and Sue was that now we were all going to live in homes free of stress, and where Dad couldn't scare or hurt us anymore or fight with Ma in the middle of the night. Being apart from each other and living such a long way away was the painful part. Regardless of what I felt or thought, they were catching the train to Texas at midnight, and Bernie and I were moving in with

Sue and Jim. It may have been exciting for Pat, but it certainly was hell for me.

Ma, always being the chronicler of our family through her letter writing, continued to do so while they were living in Texas. We loved reading her letters and knowing what was going on with them. My sister-in-law Karoline always had her camera ready so we could get a sense of life in Texas through her many photos. I can still remember Pat and Danny in their uniforms with ties that they wore to the military-style school they went to on the Air Force base. The photos depicted a happy lifestyle for them all. It was an event each time a letter would arrive. Sue would read the letters out loud to whoever was around. Ma provided us with detailed descriptions of life on the Brooks Air Force base. Sadly, none of these descriptive letters survived. However, what we do have are my memories of the changes my family went through and how the rupture and subsequent move impacted each of us. We missed Ma, Danny, and Pat a great deal. Sometimes, the letters and photos made us all very sad.

I was close with all my siblings, and we interacted a lot throughout our lives. The trauma and excitement of that New Year's Eve was frequently revisited at family gatherings. We all saw it as a sad time of forced separation but ended up seeing that it had been good for us all and, surprisingly, even for Dad. In retrospect, it was a reprieve from the toxic stress. It was eight months of lessened tension, anxiety, and periodic terror for us all. But it certainly was a good respite for all except for Sue and Jim and Karoline and Tommy. These two young couples took us in and increased their responsibilities overnight. It certainly was challenging for them, but also very kind of them to open their homes to us. We were more desperate than I realized, and they rescued us. I suspect that we inadvertently brought some of our toxic stress into their tranquil homes, but they handled it all admirably.

11

References

Garner AS, Shonkoff JP, Committee on Psychosocial Aspects of Child and Family Health Committee on Early Childhood, Adoption, and Dependent Care, Section on Developmental and Behavioral Pediatrics, *et al.* Early childhood adversity, toxic stress, and the role of the pediatrician: translating developmental science into lifelong health. *Pediatrics* 2012; 129: e224–31.

Onigu-Otite, Edore., & Sindhu, Idicula. (2020). Introducing ACEs (Adverse Childhood Experiences) and Resilience to First-Year Medical Students. *MedEd Portal 2020. 16:10964 http://doi.org/10.15 766/Med_2374-8265.10964*

Shonkoff JP, Gamer AS, Granger DA, Dobbins MI, et al. The Science of Early Life Toxic Stress for Pediatric and Advocacy. *Pediatrics* 2013: 131:319-27.

Chapter 2

ACEs, PACEs, Pat, and Me

While reviewing the sequence of events that led me to discover ACEs, my wife Janice and I concluded that the way I came upon ACEs was a "God Thing." Let me explain. Each year, our local library runs a sale of used books, and we usually take advantage of it. This past fall of 2022 was no exception, but this time it was significantly different. The book sale is usually a very orderly and friendly affair, but not this year. Right away, I sensed a difference while in the lobby, waiting for the doors to open and the sale to begin. I noticed six or eight people huddled together and speaking a language I did not understand, but their facial expressions were ones of seriousness and focused intensity. Unlike the rest of us carrying shopping bags, they each were holding a somewhat large plastic bin.

When the doors opened, the serious and intense people pushed past the rest of us and dispersed throughout the room. They all wore computer gadgets of some sort on their wrists that they referred to frequently. They also consulted with each other on some books before placing them in their bins. For some crazy reason, their intensity spread to me, and I became nervous and eager to find books to purchase before they got them. I am usually selective when looking for books in some selected genres, but not tonight. Within 20 minutes, I selected (snatched?) a dozen or so books after only a cursory scrutiny of each. The intense people were still busy filling their bins. It was like they were gathering as many books as possible to get a library started in some distant land. What else could it be? Who knows?

On the way home, Janice and I shared our feelings and agreed that it was the most harrowing book-shopping experience of our lives. Regardless, when I got home, I found that I had selected some great books amidst the chaos and have now read all that I bought that night. Now comes the God Thing. One of those books that I ended up with had an unusual title: *Hillbilly Elegy*. However, I think it was the subtitle that caught my eye: *A Memoir of a Family and Culture in Crisis*. I love reading memoirs, and as a one-time anthropology major, anything about cultures is another subject that I gravitate toward. No matter what, I had the pleasure of reading a great book that I highly recommend, but that's not the point. The point is that this book opened my eyes, my mind, and my heart to ACEs (Adverse Childhood Experiences), and the more I learn about ACEs, the more impressed I become.

Finding this book amidst the chaos was the God Thing because it gave me the focus I needed in order to write this book about my brother Pat. With about 30 or 40 pages left to read in *Hillbilly Elegy*, on page 226 was a description and a list that changed my life. Vance (the author) defines ACEs as "Adverse Childhood Experiences that are "traumatic childhood events, and their consequences reach far into adulthood. The trauma need not be physical." (Vance, 2016) When I read this, I immediately thought of Pat's early life and the rest of us kids growing up poor with an alcoholic dad, loads of toxic stress, and lacking in everyday things other kids had like nice clothes, plenty to eat, two supportive parents, cars, vacations, toys, sports equipment, and on and on.

Vance goes on to list some of the most common ACEs:

- "Being sworn at, insulted, or humiliated by parents.
- Being pushed, grabbed, or having something thrown at you.
- Feeling that your family didn't support each other.
- Having parents separated or divorced.
- Living with an alcoholic or drug user.

14

- Living with someone who was depressed or attempted suicide.
- Watching a loved one abused."

There are three more ACEs that are on the complete ACEs test, but these are the only ones Vance included in his book. You will see the complete list if you do what I suggest you do in my note below:

Note: I recommend that you get your own ACEs score by taking the ten-question test in Appendix A of this book. It is only ten yes or no questions. I also recommend you do what I did: take the test again and pretend you are someone you know who had a difficult childhood. Be sure not to share the results with anyone, especially the person you pretended to be. This may cause them to be hurt or angry and feel somewhat used in some way without you obtaining their permission. If you can use someone you had known well but who has since died, you will avoid this pitfall.

Now, set your two ACEs test scores aside, and let's move on. Going back to Vance and my "God Thing" journey, he answers the "so what question" people often have when they first hear about ACEs. "Children with multiple ACEs are more likely to struggle with anxiety and depression, to suffer from heart disease and obesity, and to contract certain types of cancers. They're also more likely to underperform in school and suffer from relationship instability as adults."

Acting as if I were Pat taking the ACEs test, he and I both got very high ACEs scores (6 out of 10 for him and 7 out of 10 for me). We both also had every one of the conditions Vance lists above. That was my eureka moment and God Thing that gave me the focus I needed to tell Pat's sad and unusual life story.

So, if ACEs are the Adverse (or negative) Childhood Experiences, what are PACEs, and what is PACEs science? I can answer both questions using information from some of the ACEs-related research findings that are quite vast and very solid.

What is PACEs science?

The science of PACEs refers to the research about the stunning effects of positive and adverse childhood experiences (PACEs) and how they work together to affect our lives, as well as our organizations, systems, and communities. It comprises:

1. **The CDC and Kaiser-Permanente study:** The Centers for Disease Control and Prevention-Kaiser Permanente ACE Study: and subsequent surveys that show that most people in the U.S. have at least one ACE and that people with four ACEs— including living with an alcoholic parent, racism, bullying, witnessing violence outside the home, physical abuse, and losing a parent to divorce — have a huge risk of adult onset of chronic health problems such as heart disease, cancer, diabetes, suicide, and alcoholism. There are three categories that together comprise a total of 10 ACEs:
   Abuse: Physical, Emotional, and Sexual,
   Neglect: Physical and Emotional,
   Household Dysfunction: Mental Illness, Mother treated violently, Divorce, Incarcerated relative, and Substance abuse. This landmark study in 2019 demonstrated that the more ACEs experienced before the age of 19, the greater the risk of dying from five of the top 10 leading causes of death.
   There are now decades of research linking ACEs to an increased risk of developing chronic diseases, depression, and alcoholism. It has also been recently demonstrated that a correlation between ACEs and an increased risk for prescription opioid misuse.
   Also, multiple ACEs put individuals at a greater risk for <u>negative outcomes,</u> including poor school

performance, unemployment, and the development of high-risk health behaviors, such as smoking and drug use. "A person with 4 or more ACES is:

2.4 times more likely to have a stroke.

1.9 times more likely to have cancer.

12 times more likely to attempt suicide.

7 times more likely to develop alcoholism." (remember Pat's ACES score was 6, and mine was 7).

Disconcerting numbers, of course, but there are things known as Mitigating Circumstances that can lower the risks for negative outcomes that will be described in detail in the next chapter.

2. **Brain science (neurobiology of toxic stress): toxic stress caused by ACEs damages the function and structure of kids' developing brains:** While nearly everyone experiences stress, chronic stress sustained over time can damage the body and the brain, especially for children, because early childhood is critical for development. ACEs cause toxic stress and prolonged or excessive activation of the stress response system. (Sadly, Pat and I grew up in a toxic, stress-filled home that put us both above the norm for ACEs and below the norm for PACEs).

3. **Results of a study of how ACEs are reflected in the mental health of adults:** Relatedly, two research physicians (Julia L. Herzog and Christian Schmahl) at the Central Institute for Mental Health, University of Heidelberg in Mannheim, Germany, reviewed the existing literature on neurobiology, mental and somatic (bodily) health in later adulthood and summarized the results for a concise qualitative overview with their results published in the Frontiers in Psychiatry. Herzog and Schmahl confirmed that in adulthood, the history of ACEs can result in complex clinical profiles with several co-occurring mental and somatic disorders such as posttraumatic stress disorder,

depression, borderline personality disorder, obesity, and diabetes. (Herzog & Schmahl, 2018).

4. **Health consequences**: toxic stress caused by ACEs affects short- and long-term health and can impact every part of the body, leading to autoimmune diseases, such as arthritis, as well as heart disease, breast cancer, lung cancer, etc.

5. **Historical and generational trauma: epigenetic consequences of toxic stress**: (Epigenetics is the study of how our behaviors and environment can cause changes that affect the way our genes work).

   Unlike genetic changes, epigenetic changes are reversible and do not change your DNA sequence, but they can change how your body reads a DNA sequence). Toxic stress caused by ACEs can alter how our DNA functions and how that can be passed on from generation to generation.

6. **Positive Childhood Experiences (PACEs) and resilience research and practice**: Here is some good news. Building on the knowledge that the brain is plastic and the body wants to heal, this part of PACEs science includes evidence-based practice, as well as practice-based evidence by people, organizations and communities that are integrating trauma-informed and resilience-building practices. This ranges from looking at how the brain of a teen with a high ACE score can be healed with cognitive behavior therapy to how this can increase students' scores, test grades and graduation rates. This is where my brother Pat's life and lifestyle diverged from mine, and how this came to be is detailed in the upcoming chapter entitled Resilience or Hardiness.

7. Bethel et al. conducted an extensive statewide investigation using the Behavioral Risk Factor Survey in Wisconsin that demonstrated how PCEs impact adult mental and relational health.

What are the Consequences of ACEs, and What is Supportive Research?

1. Adverse Childhood Experiences (ACEs) harm children's developing brains and lead to changing how they respond to stress and damaging their immune systems so profoundly that the effects show up decades later. ACEs cause much of our burden of chronic disease, most mental illnesses, and are at the root of most violence.

2. "ACEs" comes from the <u>CDC-Kaiser Adverse Childhood Experiences Study</u>, a groundbreaking public health study that discovered that childhood trauma leads to the adult onset of chronic diseases, depression and other mental illness, violence and being a victim of violence, as well as financial and social problems.

3. The ACE Study <u>has published about 70 research papers since 1998</u>. Hundreds of additional research papers based on the ACE Study have also been published. My most recent search using Google Scholar found 999 reports on ACEs research as of March 29, 2023. Do your own search, but do it through Google Scholar. This will result in articles from journals and books that have been reviewed by a panel of experts that validate the information before it is published. If you do the search using just Google alone, you will find opinions from newspapers, magazines, blogs, Facebook, etc., all of which are not scientifically proven evidence.

4. After the ACE Study, other ACE surveys have expanded the types of ACEs to include racism, gender discrimination, witnessing a sibling being abused, witnessing violence outside the home, witnessing a father being abused by a mother or vice versa, being bullied by a peer or adult, involvement with the foster care system, living in a war zone, living in an unsafe neighborhood, losing a family member to deportation, etc.

(Our dad was a racist, and Pat was bullied or pummeled by us all throughout his young life, so these could conceivably be added to his ACEs score).

5. *The ACEs study found a direct link between childhood trauma and adult onset of chronic disease, incarceration, and employment challenges. The higher the number of ACEs, the greater the incident of negative outcomes.* The following study both shocked and inspired me because of its relevancy to Pat and his epilepsy: Anto, Shipley, et al. recently published their results of a study of ACEs and epilepsy or seizures that was very relevant to my brother Pat. It appeared in 2023 in the journal of Neurology of Clinical Practice (Anto, Shipley, Massey, and Szperka, March 10, 2023) entitled: *ACEs Are Associated with Seizure in Children: A Cross-sectional Analysis* reported research that demonstrates that adults with ACEs scores of 5 or more have an increase rate of 63% in the diagnosis of epilepsy or seizure disorder. The population studied consisted of 59,963 subjects (52.2% females and 47.8% male, ages 0-17). This was the missing link between Pat's seizures and why he had them, but back in the 1950s, when Pat was a kid, the search for a cause was in the physical realm because no one at that time knew about ACEs as a possible causative factor.

6. We know that both ACEs and PACEs do not have much of an impact unless the number of occurrences increases significantly over time. This means a small amount of adversity or love will not impact the brain, the endocrine system, and so forth but flood the kid's home environment with lots of toxic stress and adversity, and you begin to count the ACEs and anticipate the consequence when the kid becomes an adult. **PACEs, the very positive aspects of a home environment, lessen the chances of negative consequences. Scientists and researchers refer to this as**

the dose-response association. Related to the concept of dose-response, Borzelleca (2000) explains that a guy named **Paracelsus**, born in Switzerland one year before Columbus beached on American soil in 1492, coined the phrase, *"It's the dose that makes the poison."* Next time you are with friends, and you want to impress them with your knowledge of historical trivia, you can ask them if they can tell you who is known as *The Father of Toxicology* (the study of poisons), and you can then tell them it is Paracelsus! Won't they be impressed?

I want to conclude this chapter with a list of facts as a takeaway that is drawn from The National Foundation to End Child Abuse and Neglect. The following facts have been proven to be true:

1. **ACEs are common.** About 61% of adults surveyed across 25 states reported they had experienced at least one type of ACE before age 19, and nearly 1 in 6 reported they had experienced four or more types of ACEs.

2. **Preventing ACEs could potentially reduce many health conditions.** For example, by preventing ACEs, up to 1.9 million heart disease cases and 21 million depression cases could have been potentially avoided.

3. **Some children are at greater risk than others.** Women and several racial/ethnic minority groups were at greater risk for experiencing four or more types of ACEs.

4. **ACEs are costly.** The economic and social costs to families, communities, and society totals hundreds of billions of dollars each year. A 10% reduction in ACEs in North America could equate to an annual savings of $56 billion.

5. If you are still skeptical about the validity of ACEs, I encourage you to skim this article that was published in the esteemed British publication The Lancet Public Health, Volume 2, Issue 8, August 2017, pages e256 – e366. Look for this article entitled:

The Effect of Multiple Adverse Childhood Experiences on Health: A Systematic Review and Meta-Analysis by Hughes, K., and Bellis, M., et al. Be prepared to see the titles of a multitude of research articles that validate ACEs from many perspectives.

6. **Lastly, a significant examination of the validity of ACEs from several statistical perspectives by Mei., Li, ZS, et al. and is included in the following comprehensive study of ACEs:**

Background

Utilizing Adverse Childhood Experiences (ACEs) measurement scales to assess youths' adversities has expanded exponentially in health and justice studies. However, most of the ACEs assessment scales have yet to meet critical psychometric standards, especially for key demographic and minority groups. It is critical that any assessment or screening tool is not reinforcing bias, warranting the need for validating ACEs tools that are equitable, reliable and accurate. The current study aimed to examine the structural validity of an ACEs scale. Using data from the 2019 Behavioral Risk Factor Surveillance System (BRFSS), which collected 97,314 responses collected from adults across sixteen states. This study assessed the psychometric properties and measurement invariance of the ACEs tool under the structural equation modeling framework.

Results

We found the 11-item ACEs screening tool as a second-order factor with three subscales, all of which passed the measurement invariance tests at metric and scalar levels across age, race, sex, socioeconomic status, gender identity, and sexual orientation. We also found that minority groups experienced more childhood adversity with a small effect size, except for gender identity.

Conclusion

The ACEs measurement scale from the BRFSS is equitable and free from measurement bias regardless of one's age, race, sex, socioeconomic status, gender identity, and sexual orientation, and thus is valid to be used to compare group mean differences within these groups. The scale is a potentially valid, viable, and predictive risk assessment in health, justice, and research settings to identify high-risk groups or individuals for treatments.

References

Anto, Shipley, Massey, & Szperka). *ACEs Are Associated with Seizures in Children: A Cross-sectional Analysis.* Neurology of Clinical Practice, (March 10, 2023).

Bethel, C., Jones, J., Gombojav, N., Linkenbach, J., & Sage, R., (2019), *Positive Childhood Experiences and Adult Mental and Relational Health in a Statewide Sample: Across Adverse Childhood Experiences Levels.* JAMA Pediatrics, Nov., 173 (11);193007.

Borzelleca, J.F. *Paracelsus: Herald of Modern Toxicology.* Toxicological Sciences. (Volume 53, Issue 1, January 2000)

Brown, AD, Anda RF, Tiemeier H, et al. *Adverse Childhood Experiences and the Risk of Premature Mortality.* American Journal of Preventive Medicine (2009: 37: 389-96).

Bucci, M., Marques, SS, Oh D, & Harris. NB. *Toxic Stress in Children and Adolescents.* Advances in Pediatrics, (2016: 63: 403 28).

Hughes, K., Bellis, M., et al. *The Effect of Multiple Adverse Childhood Experiences on Health: A Systematic Review and Meta-analysis.* The Lancet Public Health (Volume 2, Issue 8, August 2017, pages e356-e366).

Mei, X., Li, J., Li, ZS. *et al. Psychometric evaluation of an Adverse Childhood Experiences (ACEs) measurement tool: an equitable assessment or reinforcing biases. Health Justice* 10, 34 (2022). https://doi.org/10.1186/s40352-022-00198-2.The information for this chapter was drawn from The National Foundation to End

Child Abuse and Neglect *Unwrapping the Link Between Childhood Trauma and Health.* (Http://www.endcan.org)

Vance, J.D. (2016), *Hillbilly Elegy.* HarperCollins Publishers.

Chapter 3

Hail Sobriety!

Returning to the days of "our family's rupture "and the aftermath of Dad's return home to find an empty flat was not the end for Dad; it was a new beginning. Rather than say he "saw the light," it may be better to say that he was struck by a bolt of lightning!

Perhaps it was the empty flat that was the impetus that caused my Dad to embrace sobriety. Certainly, the sequence of the following events facilitated the change. Our aunt, who lived upstairs from us and was also our landlady, relayed what happened to Dad that awful night. Apparently, in his drunken state, he tried to enter the wrong house. When he turned to leave, he fell down the stairs and cut himself badly on the broken bottles of beer he was carrying. Fortunately, the people living in the house that Dad tried to enter called my aunt, who also happened to be a Registered Nurse. She bandaged Dad as best she could but realized that his many cuts needed sutures. So, her husband (my Dad's brother) took him to Mercy Hospital, where he was stitched up and admitted. He remained in the hospital for about three or four weeks. During that time, he went through detoxification and called my sister Sue, looking for Ma. The real shock came when he found out about Ma's stealthy escape to Texas. Dad pleaded with Sue to visit him in the hospital. So, Sue and Jim visited first, and then Bernie and I went to see him every day after school, which was located right behind the hospital. Dad sure was a different person from the guy I was used to seeing. He was friendly and kind (he saved his dessert for me every day) and was interested in what we did in school like Bernie playing drums in the band. I realize now that until then, I could not remember ever seeing him sober and not mean like he was when he wasn't drinking. He sure was a different guy. I liked this guy.

Unfortunately, when it was time for Dad to be discharged from the hospital, he had no place to go. Out of desperation, he asked his son-in-law Jim if he could come to live with all of us in their new home that Sue and Jim had just moved into. Jim said Dad could live there, but there could be no more drinking. He also said that Dad had to work steadily, and the only place he had for him to sleep was in their unfinished attic. Dad agreed to all of Jim's conditions and moved into what he humorously called his "garret."

During the next six months or so, Ma and Dad reconciled through letter writing and phone calls. This brought forth both joy and concern throughout the family about the permanence of Dad's newfound sobriety and many bad memories of how he used to be. Regardless, we all needed and wanted to be back together, and Sue and Jim needed us gone so they could have their home and lives back.

I was very much aware of the ways Dad had changed. He, of course, was no longer drinking, which was significant because he also was no longer dispensing toxic stress. I was generating my own toxic stress as I struggled hopelessly with my math homework. I was shocked when Dad volunteered to help me. He showed kindness and patience, and he did help me.

Dad also took pride in his being able to work as much overtime as possible. The extra income enabled him to pay off some creditors, like two local grocery stores where we had charged a great deal. Each time he got a charge account eliminated, he proudly showed me the "Paid in Full" note. It was great to have a real dad now, and I just hoped he didn't go back to drinking.

So, after eight months in Texas, Ma, Danny, and Pat joined us in Sue and Jim's new little house. This put nine of us in a two-bedroom

26

house with only one bathroom. I assumed all the adults viewed this as a short-term solution to our housing problem that was severely exacerbated by Pat. He was very jealous of Sue and Jim's daughter Kathleen and threw outrageous tantrums whenever she got something and he didn't. During those times, he was inconsolable. The whole household was in a collective state of angst as Pat wailed away without restraint. After too many of these episodes, Sue asked Ma to move out, and who could blame her? Interestingly, I do not recall Ma saying that Pat threw tantrums in Texas. Did this mean that Pat could show some restraint? Were the tantrums we witnessed only because of the rage he felt toward Kathleen? None of us were sure.

So, now, the search for a new place for us to live was accelerated. Eventually, Ma and Dad found a trailer that they could afford to purchase. This would be their first and only venture into home ownership. It was in a "Trailer Camp" located in Lackawanna, NY, where Ma and Dad grew up and where Ma still had some friends.

It also was within commuting distance via two buses to Dad's railroad engineer's job. The trailer was kind of small for two adults and three kids (Bernie elected to stay with Sue and Jim in order to finish high school in Buffalo). It was only 35 feet in length and less than 8 feet in width. However, we saw it as cozy, and we all loved it, especially Pat.

The only downside of trailer camp living was that Pat was still unable to make friends, just as it was in our old neighborhood. In contrast, Danny and I quickly made friends, but we intentionally excluded Pat because he was unwilling to cooperate or ever just go with the flow. Everything had to be his way or else he would scream and cry. That is exactly what we wanted to avoid. We did not want to be shunned by our newfound friends. They were the most adventurous and fun friends we ever had. They feared nothing, nor did I. We hopped freight trains, hiked deep into unfamiliar woods, rode homemade rafts down swollen spring creeks, hitched rides on the bumpers of cars and trucks in winter, and in winter, recklessly rode pieces of metal like sleds down very steep icy hills. Danny showed more caution than I did, which was a good thing, and because of Pat's attitude and tantrums, he was not allowed to join in our reckless fun. His tantrums never really bothered Danny and me because we were much faster than Pat, and we just ran off when he started screaming. A form of pummeling? Oh, yes! I still have lots of guilt about those days shunning Pat in those trailer camp times, even today.

Regardless, what Pat especially enjoyed about trailer camp living was our non-drinking Dad. He was very different in general, but especially toward Pat. Much kinder. More patient and tolerant. He was dispensing PACEs freely and never knew the good he was doing. Ma worked from 7:00 a.m. to 3:00 p.m. in Central Supply in a local hospital, and Dad worked from 4:00 p.m. to 12:00 a.m. Their work schedules provided my brothers and me with the supervision we sorely needed but resented greatly. The three of us were doing poorly in school and were always seeking the next adventure, whether within or outside of our parents' rules. Our antics drove my Dad crazy, but surprisingly, it did not drive him to drink. This showed how solid his commitment to not drinking really was.

To his credit, Dad achieved his non-drinking lifestyle without the support of AA or any other kinds of therapy and interventions. Very impressive!

This new Dad was something to behold. He worked steadily at his well-paying job as a railroad engineer, brought his pay home, cleaned and straightened the trailer each day, made our lunches, went grocery shopping with another engineer who had a car (we did not), did repairs on the trailer, interacted with other men in the trailer camp community, visited our school to see how we were doing academically and behaviorally (poorly on both counts for the three of us), and he did his best to parent us. It was a valiant effort, but I suspect the results were far from what he expected. Regardless, he soldiered on in this unfamiliar role as a dad as best he could.

Having had personal and professional experience with alcoholism, I know what it took for Dad to undergo the transformation he experienced without the help of AA or any treatment program. It is a most challenging transition to stop drinking and becoming sober. In general, some people stop drinking but are angry and miserable. AA would refer to such a person as a "Dry Drunk." This was not Dad. Andrew Brevin, a Voluntary Mentor at the OAD Clinic in London, UK, captures the difference in a personal message he sent out to those going through this transition, "There is a fundamental difference between not drinking and living sober…. Living sober is different from simply not drinking." As I read Andrew's insightful message, I can see my Dad: "It's a commitment to living one's life differently. It's about attitude, commitment, habit, practice and who you mix with. The chances of sustained recovery are far greater if you can bring about meaningful changes in your life rather than adopting an attitude that not drinking is a burden that deprives you in some way." This was our new Dad. (Bevan, The OAD Clinic, May 9, 2022).

In summary, Andrew Bevan provides a message that captures my Dad's transition perfectly: "Living sober is more than just not drinking – it's about finding a new sense of hope and purpose in life, new practices, and new sources of enjoyment that share your outlook on life." Dad found all this in his family, our trailer camp community, his work, his pride in fixing things, the pleasure of meeting new people and socializing, and trying to be the best husband and dad possible. I am proud that my Dad achieved sobriety, and he did it his way.

Certainly, Dad's sober way of living precluded his spreading toxic stress around. In fact, he continued his supportive way and tried to be a better parent and husband. However, he came up against three disrespectful and uncooperative sons: Danny, Pat, and me. In his own way, he was trying to provide us with support and nurturance, but we were not responding well, and he was not very patient with the process.

As I said above, Dad did not have a rich reservoir of parenting knowledge and skills, and Pat could manipulate him quite easily. He felt sorry for Pat because he did not have any friends. His solution was to give Pat extra money to buy toys, ice cream cones, candy, model planes and cars, or anything either of them could think of. When Dad dispensed love and concern for Pat, shrewd Pat saw opportunities and seized them.

Because Pat had no friends, he spent a lot of his time in the trailer with Ma and Dad or went socializing with them in the trailer camp community. Also, if they were invited to another couple's trailer for an evening to play cards or just to socialize, they always took Pat with them. These couples did not have kids for Pat to play with, so I assume Pat was bored. Despite that, he was always eager to tag along because he always got plenty of snacks.

Regardless of the motivations engendered by Pat and Dad, they bonded in a somewhat tenuous way. I think Dad pitied Pat and perhaps felt guilty about his years of drinking and neglect of the family that, of course, included Pat. Swimming provides an ideal example of how he tried to prevent Pat from being sad and lonely.

Danny and I, along with our friends, swam in a nearby creek about a mile from our trailer. We never invited Pat because he could not swim very well, and our friends would shun us if we brought him along. Also, the creek was no place for Pat to swim because it was over his head and had a swift current. There were, of course, great tantrums whenever we announced that we were going swimming. Ma and Dad knew the dangers of the creek, and so they did not press us to take Pat. Dad took a different approach. He ordered, delivered, bought, and assembled Pat's own little swimming pool. It was only one foot deep, eight feet square, but was well constructed with a canvas liner and a metal tubular frame with seats in each corner. I remember watching them work together congenially until the assembly went awry. With that, Pat was having his typical meltdown while Dad kept a cooler head and persevered. Finally, the pool was assembled, and Dad had the hose filling it up while Pat put on his swimsuit. Then came the great pool crisis!

One thing the trailer came with was very, very cold spring water, regardless of the outside temperature. Now we have two very sad people: Pat was trying to get in the cold pool while simultaneously screaming and crying about the extremely cold water, while Dad hustled back and forth, bringing hot water that was boiling on the stove in three or four pans. Of course, this was all in vain due to simple physics: the volume of very cold water in the pool was far greater than twenty-plus pots of boiling water could alter. Kudos to Dad for hanging in there and for not abandoning his hard-earned commitment to not drinking. He instead showed great patience and love. Quite amazing. Eventually, the water became comfortable for Pat, and he swam about in his little pool.

Here is another example of Pat's manipulation of Dad and Dad's coddling of Pat. For some reason, Ma and Dad did something unexpected when we first moved into the trailer. They enrolled Danny, Pat, and me in a Catholic grammar school that was about one mile away. It was a brutal walk on blustery, freezing winter days up a long hill that we all dreaded. Knowing what was ahead, Danny and I just did the unavoidable and took off as soon as we were bundled up while Pat stayed in bed, ignoring Dad's pleading and mild, very mild threats. What enraged Danny and me as we trudged up the windy hill on the way to school would be Pat smiling broadly out the bus window and waving as it whisked on by. We felt betrayed whenever Dad would give Pat money for the bus while we raged on to each other with every step. If the physical pummeling of Pat was permitted, Danny and I would be first in line.

In those days, I knew Dad was disgusted with Danny, Pat, and me because we were all doing so poorly in school, ignored rules at home and in the trailer camp, and really did not care about the consequences. There were no incentives or threats that would get us to study, complete assignments, or follow any rules. In school, we were also interfering with the learning of the other students because we were so rowdy and disruptive in class.

I don't really know what the straw was that broke my Dad's back (figuratively), but he suddenly transferred us out of the Catholic school, where he had to pay tuition and put us in the free public school. It was a shock to us to be transferred after just one year and a month, but we would not miss the uniforms we had to wear with ties nor the strictness of the nuns. Dad foolishly supported us and yelled at the Principal, "You should be ashamed to wear the habit."

Yelling at a nun? And she was also the Principal! I don't know what precipitated that outburst, but I could hear him yell that blasphemous insult through the sliding doors that separated my classroom from the Principal's.

Going to the public school provided us with activities like gym, art, woodshop, music, etc., that broke up the tedium of constant classwork. We needed diversion and generated our own if it was not available to us. The teachers probably called us the "terrible Talty trio" or some other justified label.

It was Pat's peers, both in the trailer camp and at school, who were now his "primary pummelers." Sadly, this was augmented by family members, including myself. He was such an easy target and inadvertently provided ample opportunities for ridicule and criticism. Only Dad did not participate in what I call the "pile-on-Pat pummelings." Dad even intervened and protected Pat whenever

32

he could. The pummeling of Pat was certainly unintentionally exacerbated by his teachers because his schoolwork was either not done or was done so poorly that he was constantly under threat of failing whatever grade he was in. We often loved to recall that he did, in fact, failed Kindergarten! We ignored the fact that it was routine back in the early '50s to place students who were not ready for First grade in what was known as "First Primer" to help "catch them up." Below is his First Primer teacher's note "promoting" Pat into First grade:

June 20, 1952

Patrick Talty has completed the work of the First Primer Class and is ready to begin the work of the First Grade. Here is the proof and it was signed by his teacher.

Schoolwork remained a problem for Pat because of his undiagnosed AD/HD (see the next chapter). Despite that, it seems there were two factors that enabled him to progress through each grade of Grammar School despite inadequate performance in the classroom. These were what they called "The On Condition System" and his size. The On Condition System allowed a kid to progress to the next grade with the understanding that inadequate performance in the next grade could cause them to be returned to the original grade. (Danny and I, along with Pat, were passed "On Condition" throughout most of our Grammar School years, but none of us were ever sent back. (It was probably a false threat.). The second reason Pat was moved on (according to Ma) was that he had gained a great deal of weight and was the biggest kid in his class. He was fat, but I doubt this really played a part in the decision to promote him. Ma always had her own view of things.

I reviewed some of Pat's Report Cards and could see he was essentially a C student and that his best work was in Mathematics, where he usually earned a B. He earned D's in Spelling and had Unsatisfactory ratings in these behavioral parameters:

- *Begins work promptly.*
- *Usually makes best effort.*
- *Refrains from unnecessary talking in class and hall.*
- *Listens politely when someone is talking.*
- *Works and plays well with others.*

The traits above, coupled with his poor academic performance are consistent with the Attention Deficit/Hyperactive Disorder (A-D/HD) diagnosis, and this will be explained fully in the next chapter.

Pat's childhood was a lonely and sad one. Whatever we were doing with friends in the trailer camp or in other neighborhoods where we lived, Pat was vigorously or surreptitiously excluded by Danny and me, as well as our friends. If a group of us built a tree fort in the woods behind the trailer camp, made a raft to float down the little creek near us, had a campfire with a potato roast, or played a baseball game, sadly, Pat could only watch from afar.

There were times when he would try to imitate what we were doing, but usually with disastrous results like his sinking raft or his potato roast, where his out-of-control campfire led to the destruction of a large section of our beloved woods.

These events provided much fodder for recall and ridicule of Pat for many years. Much non-physical pummeling followed each of his failures and was retold many times thereafter. We were a sick bunch, and regrettably, I often led the" pummeling pack."

During these days, Ma was also struggling in trying to get us to do our homework and to follow the rules, but she was too tired when she arrived home around the same time that we did. As a result, she let things slide. She also had to make dinner, do the dishes, and take care of the other household chores that Dad didn't get to do. I think she was also just too tired to try to enlist our help. The same thing applied to our homework. We only wanted to play outside or watch TV. What a bunch!

Reference

Bevan, Andrew (May 9, 2022) *Living Sober Versus Not Drinking* The OAD Clinic, London, United Kingdom.

Chapter 4

Pat's Learning Disability

In 1960, Pat was attending his seventh grammar school, and to add to this challenge, he had a history of not adapting well to change. Today, the occupational therapist in me sees a learning disability in Pat along the lines of A-D/HD (Attention-Deficit/Hyperactivity Disorder), but back in the 1950s and early 1960s, when Pat was struggling through all those grammar schools, this condition was just beginning to be identified. However, looking back, I can see Pat having many of the symptoms of A- D/HD (see below), and like thousands of other kids in those days, it went unidentified and thus untreated. Also, like many other kids with A-D/HD, I think Pat had above average functional intelligence. I base this on my frequent observations of him as he analyzed and attempted various ways to resolve the many complexities and adversities he encountered in life.

It was in 1968 that the American Psychiatric Association (APA) included the diagnosis of *Hyperkinetic Reaction of Children,* which was a precursor to A-D/HD, in the second edition of the American Psychiatric Association's "Bible" the DSM-V (*Diagnostic and Statistical Manual of Mental Disorders,* 2022). The DSM is now in its 5th edition, and despite some critics, the diagnosis of A-D/HD is securely ensconced as a diagnosis in this highly regarded publication. That being what it is, Pat's lackluster classroom performance, immature behavior, and poor ability to manage stress all suggest that if he were a student enrolled in today's educational system, I do not doubt that he would have been readily evaluated and diagnosed with A-D/HD. Below, I include all of the criteria for the diagnosis of A-D/HD, as specified in the DSM-V, specifically the Inattention type of A-D/HD, and Pat has consistently demonstrated every one of them throughout his grammar school years and into adulthood:

- Often fails to give close attention to details or makes careless mistakes.
- Often has difficulty sustaining attention in tasks or play activities.
- Often does not seem to listen when spoken to directly.
- Often does not follow through on instructions and fails to finish schoolwork, chores, or duties in the workplace.
- Often has difficulty organizing tasks or activities.
- Is often easily distracted by extraneous stimuli.
- Is often forgetful in daily activities.

Although he certainly does fit the criteria above for the diagnosis of Inattention- Disorder, looking back at my observations of him through the lens of an experienced developmental occupational therapist, I did not see the symptoms of the disorder of Hyperactivity/Impulsivity below, nor do I recall his teachers or Ma reporting any of these behaviors:

- Often fidgets with or taps hands or feet or squirms in his seat.
- Often leaves seat in situations when remaining seated is expected.
- Often runs about or climbs in situations where it is inappropriate.
- Often unable to play or engage in leisure activities quietly.
- Is often "on the go," acting as if "driven by a motor."
- Often blurts out an answer before a question has been completed.
- Often has difficulty waiting his or her turn.

Pat most definitely did not demonstrate the symptoms that go along with the Hyperactivity/Impulsivity form of A-D/HD. Rather than Pat being hyperactive/impulsive, he was lethargic. His lethargy could be due to the medications he was on to control his seizures, the residual effects of a severe seizure, his sedentary lifestyle, and/or the 150# that he weighed in the eighth grade.

Pat's A-D/HD made schoolwork impossible for him. This is not to say he didn't try. His confidence was limited, his efforts were inadequate, and, of course, the results were poor. Consequently, he was pummeled to excess throughout his life and was knocked down repeatedly. However, he always got back up and tried his best to carry on. He just did not have the tools.

Below are two letters of Ma's that describe some academic success Pat experienced and, conversely, his poor emotional maturity and limited frustration tolerance. Ma even ponders institutionalizing Pat.

P.S. Patrick is getting worse every day, not in health but in his actions concerning Kathleen. He doesn't have a friend in the world, and he is so jealous of Kathleen it isn't funny. He thinks he should go with Sue and Kathleen every time they go out. He cries if he can't. Yesterday, he went all to pieces and went after her. I was afraid he would kill her if we hadn't been around. After a while, he went upstairs, and she called him "jerky." He came down the stairs, livid with rage; I had to holler to Peter, and Pat kept saying, "I'll kill her" over and over. Sue gets so upset with him that she tells him to shut up and mind his own business. I know she doesn't mean it, but that's the way things are here. Maybe he would be better off away someplace or maybe I should take him to a Psychiatrist. I can't spell it, but you know what I mean.

Although Pat's home environment is not what he needs, Ma describes how the transfer to a different school (his seventh) has been beneficial for him but with the usual glitches:

September 22 (Pat's Birthday) 1959

Pat seems to like School #28. I told you before he has a man teacher and is taking Industrial Arts. He loves to build, so he should enjoy that. He also asked me if he could take drum lessons, but I said no, so he told the teacher (music) that he would take trumpet lessons. I told him that I couldn't afford to buy him one, and he said, "They only cost $130, and you never have money for anything." But I know him like a book because it would be a fascination for him for a while, then he would be sick of it. So, I say, let him use one of the trumpets over at school, when he decides to really play and stick to it, I wouldn't mind buying him one. Dan would like to take piano lessons, but he must straighten out in school before I undertake that project. Of course, a piano is up my alley, you know that.

Sadly, Pat was born too late to have benefitted from the interventions for A-D/HD that are commonplace in the school systems today. I spent ten years working in several schools as an occupational therapist where kids like Pat were identified early on by their teachers, speech pathologists, or occupational therapists (like me) and then coordinated systems of interventions were put in place that helped these kids catch up developmentally with their peers.

I must wonder what this established system of professional evaluations and a plan of intervention could have done for Pat academically, developmentally, and interpersonally.

I now see that many of our frustrations as a family with Pat and the subsequent pummelings we administered were the result of his inability to cope and adapt because of his undiagnosed (until now)

A-D/HD. Keep this burden of his in mind as we look further into Pat's life.

Pat had other burdens that were neither identified nor addressed at any time in his troubled life. For me to present these other burdens, I need to bring in some concepts that explain his behavior and his difficulties in adulthood from a different perspective. The next few chapters will provide the background to help appreciate some other aspects of Pat's difficult life.

References

American Psychiatric Association (2022). *Diagnostic and Statistical Manual of Mental Disorders* (5th edition).

Falvo, DR, Holland, BE (2018). *Medical and Psychosocial Aspects of Chronic Illness and Disability.* Jones & Bartlett Learning.

Chapter 5

A More Detailed Comparison of ACE Scores:

Pat's and Mine

I include a comparison between Pat and myself using information from each of our ACEs and the subsequent physical and mental health difficulties that one or both of us experienced as adults. Our ACEs scores (Pat with 6 and me with 7 out of 10) distinguish both of us from most people. Our scores would be considered multiple, and it would thus put both Pat and me at greater risk for the following *negative outcomes* (our first names appear next to the ones we each experienced):

Poor school performance **Pat, Peter**

Unemployment **Pat**

High-risk health behaviors such as:

> Drug use **Pat, Peter**
>
> Alcoholism **Pat, Peter**
>
> Higher BMI (Body Mass Index). Pat fell into the obesity range **Pat.**
>
> Higher Smoking Rates **Pat**
>
> Depression **Pat**

Here are some additional ACEs that were not included in the original list:

> Racism (our Dad was an overt racist). **Neither of us developed racist inclinations.**

Bullying (this is a process akin to what I am calling pummeling) **Pat.**

At different times in our lives, we were able to mitigate and, in some cases, even eliminate some of the negative outcomes of ACEs as adults, like smoking, alcohol, and drug use and the ability to become employed. However, these remaining negative outcomes continued and worsened for Pat throughout his lifetime: unemployment, obesity, heart disease, cancer, and depression. The reason I was able to avoid these as an adult had to do with the positive role models with whom I interacted throughout my adult years.

The research findings that demonstrate the link between the number of ACEs a person experienced was from a survey of 144,000 adults from 25 states (a very large and diverse sample). Sadly, Americans who had experienced even one ACE as a child before age 19 will experience negative health and behavior outcomes later in life. This all started with a 2019 study by the Centers for Disease Control and Prevention and Kaiser Permanente and is still ongoing today on multiple fronts. An extensive amount of related research can be found at '*A Decade of Science Informing Policy: The Story of the National Scientific Council on the Developing Child* Harvard University (www.developingchild.net)'. To see the scope of other research findings regarding ACEs, go to *Google Scholar* to see the array of research now published (not regular *Google).*

There are now decades of research and publications linking ACEs to an increased risk of developing chronic diseases and behavioral challenges in adulthood, including obesity, autoimmune disease, depression, and alcoholism. My siblings and I grew up in a household where ACEs were prevalent. I think it is significant that I am now the only one left out of my five siblings.

The point of ACEs applied to Pat is that there was a definite connection between Pat's Adverse Childhood Experiences (ACEs) and his problems in achieving and enjoying a full and satisfying healthy life.

I would say that Pat's surprisingly above-average intelligence, coupled with the support of Ma and our sister Sue, who were very positive influences in any success Pat experienced in his adult life.

For most of his life, Pat was seldom happy. He had a great sense of humor, but it remained unknown outside of our immediate family. He had a few years where things came together for him, but usually, he lived below the poverty line for most of his adult life, and he mostly lived it alone and was often lonely.

I remember Pat being bullied at school or at the park and him responding by fighting. He never seemed to win any of these fights because he was always so clumsy and overweight. I would sometimes take him with me back to the scene of the fight and confront the kid who had bested Pat. These kids were always much smaller and sometimes younger than Pat, so it felt strange to be ordering these kids to leave Pat alone. They just laughed. This bullying was another form of pummeling, but now it was becoming physical.

He did fail one and perhaps two grades, and that, combined with his "repeat of Kindergarten or First Primer," made him up to three years older than his peers. His struggles in grammar school finally ended when he graduated and entered High School. Unfortunately, not much had changed, and he recognized early on that the curriculum and expectations were beyond him. I suspect he anticipated more pummeling from his teachers and classmates, many of whom were his pummelers in grammar school. So, after just six weeks, and with Ma's signed approval, at the age of fifteen, Pat joined Danny and me as "high school dropouts." It was now onto his long and mostly unsuccessful search for a job.

Reference

"A Decade of Science Informing Policy: The Story of the National Scientific Council on the Developing Child. Harvard University (www.developingchild.net)

Chapter 6

Good News: Mitigating Circumstances

The research on ACEs demonstrates that because both Pat and I had high ACEs scores (his was 6 and mine was 7 out of 10), and we were both raised in a home environment rife with toxic stress, we, therefore, were at higher risk to develop these adversities or **negative outcomes** as adults:

- Social, Emotional, & Cognitive Impairment
- Adoption of Health-risk Behaviors
- Disease, Disability & Social Problems
- Early Death

The good news is that there are **mitigating circumstances** or **"protective factors"** (also known as Positive Childhood Experiences or PCEs) that can lessen the risk of anyone with higher ACEs scores (like Pat and I) developing the above negative outcomes in adulthood. The more of these protective factors below we can avail ourselves of, the more we can decrease the potential of developing the above adversities as adults. The list below was included in a study by Bethel et al. (2019), who studied a statewide sample of people with high PCEs in their adult years:

- Close relationships with competent caregivers or other caring adults (our mom and older siblings and their spouses fulfilled this need for us both).
- Parent resilience (mom had this to a large extent, but dad did not).
- Identifying and cultivating a sense of purpose (faith, culture, identity).

- Individual developmental competencies (problem-solving skills, self-regulation, agency).
- Social connections.
- Socioeconomic advantages and concrete support from parents and families.
- Communities and social systems that support health and development and nurture human capital.

*Pat and I had very different educational and work experiences once we entered young adulthood. My path enabled me to take advantage of the above protective factors in college and in my professional life as an occupational therapist, professor, spouse, father, and grandfather. In contrast, Pat had a significant learning disability (AD/HD) that went undetected, and this prevented him from being successful in academic settings. This, then, also prevented him from having access to, and the opportunities to take advantage of, these protective factors that may or may not have been available to him. I will elaborate on this in the chapter on resilience (hardiness).

Mitigating Circumstances for Pat and Me

To what extent were there PCEs (Positive Childhood Experiences or PCEs) available to Pat and me in our home and community, and to what extent did each of us avail ourselves of them? Below are the 7 PCEs that are available in homes and communities that are relatively free of toxic stress, which of course, was not our childhood home:

1. Being able to talk to our family about feelings. **Our family was not very comfortable with this, but Ma and our sister Sue provided this when we were very distraught.**
2. Feeling that our family stood by us during difficult times. **This was Ma and Sue again, but Dad was not home or interested enough to be engaged. The exception to this**

was when Dad became sober and functioned as Pat's protector and advocate in the trailer camp.

3. Enjoyed participating in community traditions. **Both Pat and I joined the Boy Scouts at different times but could not participate in going away to camp and other things that were beyond us because of our poverty.**

4. Felt a sense of belonging in high school. **Both Pat and I dropped out of high school, he after six weeks and me after three years. Neither of us felt that we belonged in high school. We differed in that I completed high school and earned both bachelor's and master's degrees.**

5. Felt supported by friends. **This was strong for me but almost nonexistent for Pat.**

6. Had at least two nonparent adults who took a genuine interest in us. **Our sister Sue and her husband Jim provided this for me, but it was quite strained with Pat for various reasons. I also had numerous mentors and colleagues who encouraged and supported me during difficult times, whereas Pat had only Ma.**

7. Felt safe and protected by an adult in our home. **Ma was our anchor and protector until her health gave way.**

Since toxic stress and poverty were so prevalent in our home life, the extent that we could draw on the above PCEs was quite limited. Prior to his becoming sober, Dad's alcoholism, gambling, and philandering engendered a life of poverty for our family, and his angry and threatening persona was a dominant presence in our home growing up.

To what extent can the lack of PCEs at home be mitigated by positive experiences in other environments like schools, the community, or even the workplace in adulthood? Three researchers at Ohio State University (Breedlove, Choi, & Zyromski) 2020 studied schools that used what they called "Restorative Practices" and demonstrated the positive difference these can make in struggling students. The mental health aspects that a child (like Pat) with ACEs combined with a lack of PCEs can be enhanced if the educational system in which they are a member employs a Restorative Practices (RP) approach. Unfortunately, Pat received the punitive approach throughout the seven grammar schools where he was enrolled.

References

Breedlove, M. Choi, J., & Zyromski, B. (2020), *Mitigating the effects of Adverse Childhood Experiences: how Restorative Practices in schools support Positive Childhood Experiences and Protective Factors:* The New Educator, DOI: 10, 1080/1547688x. 1807078.

Moran, M. *Positive Childhood Experiences May Counteract Adverse Experiences.* Published Online: 29 Oct 2019/https: 111dol.org/10:1176/Appl.pn.2019.10618.

Chapter 7

Protective Factors: Pat's versus Mine

As previously described, Pat as well as the rest of the Talty kids, grew up in a very stressful (toxic) home environment. So, if we all experienced the same toxic stress as Pat (and me), how did we turn out differently as adults? For illustration purposes and not self-glorification, I will continue to compare my life with that of Pat's. Remember, I scored a 7 out of 10 on the ACEs Questionnaire as opposed to Pat's 6 out of 10. The answer to this question lies in the research on a concept that researchers and clinicians refer to as *resilience*. This is also what the researchers on ACEs call "**Counter-ACEs.**" These counter-ACEs can lessen the negative effect of ACEs on adult health. This is significant because the landmark 1998 ACEs study concluded that individuals with four or more ACEs (like Pat and I) can develop increased levels of *resilience* if they have several of the following important individual, family, and community conditions that can support *resilience* and hence are termed "**Protective Factors:**"

- **Close relationships with competent caregivers or other caring adults**: I would put our two oldest siblings (Tommy and Sue) and their respective spouses (Karoline and Jim) as adults who fulfilled this role admirably. There was some discord between them and Pat in later years, but when we needed them the most as kids, they were there for both Pat and me.

- **Parent resilience (also known as hardiness):** I believe this was high for Ma but low for Dad. Consequently, both Pat and I were often strengthened by Ma's resilience and optimistic attitude, but this was often overshadowed by

52

Dad's negative outlook and frequent absences. Dad did, however, demonstrate some of this during his few years of sobriety prior to his early death at age 54.

- **Identifying and cultivating a sense of purpose (faith, culture, identity):** We both did this, but I did more so just because of my extended education and professional experiences.

- **Individual developmental competencies such as problem-solving skills, self-regulation, and agency (agency is the feeling of control over one's actions and their consequences):** Pat excelled at problem-solving skills, especially in the realm of mechanical problems. Self-regulation and agency were weak areas throughout his life, but far less so for me due once again to my education and association with highly successful people as role models and supportive friends, professors, supervisors, and colleagues.

- **Social connections:** Pat struggled throughout his childhood in the making of friends but got better at this as an adult. It was the reverse for me in that I always had plenty of friends throughout my childhood but, by choice, became somewhat of a social recluse in adolescence, and this continues even today. However, I mastered enough interpersonal skills to forge effective connections with mentors and helpers along the way to enjoy two successful careers as an Occupational Therapy clinician and as a professor of Occupational Therapy.

- **Socioeconomic advantages and concrete support for parents and families:** The poverty in which we were both raised precluded either one of us from being able to take advantage of this element to any extent.

- **Communities and social systems that support health and development and nurture human capital**. Pat did this on a rudimentary level, whereas I sought and utilized every opportunity that I encountered to force myself to interact with key people even though self-isolation was my wont.

Does all this mean that I did life correctly and Pat did not? "Correctly" is a highly subjective word for this hypothetical comparison in which I am engaged. A better way to compare our paths in life is that I did not have Pat's burdens of a seizure disorder, AD/HD, the inability to build friendships as a kid and adolescent, and all the consequences of living a life being pummeled. I also was able to build resilience throughout my adult life, whereas the opportunities for Pat to do this were minimal. The key difference between us is that he, unfortunately, had a far heavier load in life to bear and did not have access to all the **protective factors** that I did. It was his intelligence that enabled him to at least survive a most challenging path, and for this, I give him kudos. I doubt that I could have coped with the burdensome path he had to follow. I would have to say that one person (besides Ma) who was a protective factor for Pat would be his neurologist and neurosurgeon, Dr. Zoll, who took care of Pat for over 40 years.

Further on in Pat's and Dr. Zoll's relationship, the fact stated in Dr. Zoll's obituary that he seldom charged patients who he learned were indigent. I would say that unequivocally, Pat was indigent throughout most of his life except for the few years when he was able to earn a good living from his work either in a paint factory or as a Towmotor Driver in a warehouse. I wonder if Ma and later Pat were the beneficiaries of Dr. Zoll's largess? There is no one left who can tell us, and neither Pat nor Ma ever mentioned it to me while they were alive.

During Pat's first hospitalization after his initial seizure, it took several days for the medical staff to complete the neurological assessment, but unfortunately, the results were not definitive enough for Dr. Zoll to establish a firm cause for Pat's seizure. Pat

54

did enjoy his hospital stay (7 days?), as he states in his letter to Tommy and Karoline (see below):

1-13-57

7:30 PM

Mercy Hospital

Dear Tommy & Karoline,

How are you? I am in Mercy Hospital. I am getting along fine here in the hospital. I like the nurses. I like the food best. I'll be going home soon, but it is pretty good here. I have a friend here. His name is David Anton. Every day I go to school here. So that's all I have to say. So, goodbye from

Patrick Talty

It is interesting the things he chose to share about his hospitalization: the quality of the food, his feelings about the nurses, going to school while hospitalized, and his making a friend. Big things for a small life? Yes, but still sad.

We were all quite overwhelmed by Pat's sudden onset of a seizure disorder or epilepsy. His diagnosis, treatment options, and possible outcomes were all new and overwhelming to us. Initially, this information was not as forthcoming as Ma and the rest of us would have liked, and this was reflected in Ma's letter to Tommy below:

Jan 20, 1958

Dear Tommy & Karoline,

How are you two? I hope O.K., just anxious about Pat as we all are. We are all fine here. Today was supposed to be the verdict on Pat. As usual, I called the doctor and he said no report on either brain wave, but Pat was raising hell and giving all the nurses a hard time. So, he said if he still didn't hear, he or the hospital would call me,

55

and I could bring him home, pending the outcome of the reports. So, you see, we know as much as we did the day he went in, nothing. I asked the doctor why bring him home when he might have to go back in, and he said maybe it would calm him down a little, and I could be saving on my Blue Cross.

After Pat had been discharged from the hospital on medication to prevent future seizures hopefully, he wrote another letter to Tommy and Karoline (see below). His letters are few, but they provide some insight into his mindset and sense of self:

Patrick Talty

544 Abbott Rd

Buffalo, NY

Feb 10, 1957

Dear Tommy and Karoline,

*How are you? I am fine. I go to the YMCA every Tuesday and Friday. Thank you for the 14 dollars. I got 100 on a 50-word test. It is hanging on the blackboard. I am sitting in the first seat in the first row. (*In those days, students were seated according to their academic performance, and he must have been the best student for that week*). The temperature is 80 degrees. I go swimming every day* (this was the end of his letter, no closing).

This letter shows the highlight of his educational experience and, one in which he was understandably proud. I also had the same fifth-grade teacher (Mrs. Sauer) as Pat, and I would say she was another of the few **protective factors** in his life at that time. She was not that for me because I was unwilling to do the work she required. I was stubborn, rebellious, and uncooperative in those days.

Pat continued to have seizures that were unpredictable and oftentimes severe, and the only warning, or aura, he had was his "sick spells," where a seizure often followed that same day, but not always. His diagnosis of a seizure disorder or epilepsy was another ACE for him to carry forth into life without a ready resolution. Ma had given Pat's teacher a note from Dr. Zoll that warned them that they needed to observe Pat and let him rest when he had one of his sick spells until he felt better. His teacher was very good at sharing the notes with the school nurse and his other teachers. So, whenever he was feeling nauseous, they would take him to the Nurse's office, where he could lie down. I do not recall him being embarrassed about this special treatment, nor him complaining about his classmates making fun of him (aka, pummeling). A respite from pummeling, perhaps? I would hope so.

I do not think Pat ever had a grand mal seizure in front of his classmates or neighborhood kids. If he had, it would surely have resulted in more ridicule and pummeling. It is traumatic and very scary to witness such a seizure, and I imagine his peers would have been either terrified or entertained to see Pat in this debilitated state and would have additional entertainment if he wet himself, which he frequently did.

I don't know if it was an aura (warning) or not, but Pat would outwardly experience terror or great anxiety just prior to the onset of his seizures. His facial expression and scream were very much like a severe panic attack. Our efforts to calm him and reassure him that he was going to be okay worked most of the time, but it was Ma who was the best at calming Pat. Also, if his peers witnessed Pat in this heightened state of fear or anxiety, he would be a cruel and rare person who would not feel compassion and embarrassment for him.

References

Craig, JM, Wolff, KT, & Baglivio, MT (2022), *Clustering of adverse and positive childhood experiences: The nature and correlates of risk and protective Factors.* Child Abuse & Neglect. Volume 134 (December 2022) 10578.

Sheffield, A. & Hays-Grundo, J. (2023) *Protective and compensatory childhood experiences and their impact on adult mental health.* World Psychiatry, Feb. 22 (1): 150-151.

Chapter 8

Resilience or Hardiness

Both Pat and I were resilient or hardy, but not to the same extent. There has been quite a bit of research on resilience or hardiness (essentially synonyms), and the following summary comes from the Harvard Graduate School of Education (Shonkoff, March 2023). Jack Shonkoff is the chair of the National Scientific Council on the Developing Child, and he offers the following insights related to resilience:

- Resilience is born from the interplay between internal disposition and external experience. It derives from supportive relationships, adaptive capacities, *and* positive experiences.
- We can see and measure resilience in terms of how kids' brains, immune systems, and genes all respond to stressful experiences.
- There is a common set of characteristics that predispose children to positive outcomes in the face of adversity. Resilience is fostered in kids who have the following assets available to them:
  - o **The availability of at least one stable, caring, and supportive relationship between a child and an adult caregiver. ***
  - o A sense of mastery over life circumstances.
  - o Strong executive function and self-regulation skills.
  - o The supportive context of affirming faith or cultural traditions.

- Learning to cope with manageable threats to our physical and social well-being is critical for the development of resilience.
- Some children demonstrate greater sensitivity to both negative *and* positive experiences.
- Resilience can be situation-specific.
- **Positive and negative experiences over time continue to influence a child's mental and physical development. Resilience can be built; it's not an innate trait or a resource that can be used up. ***
- People's response to stressful experiences varies dramatically, but extreme adversity nearly always generates serious problems that require treatment.

*The highlighted two bullets above are the ones where Pat and I differ the most, and perhaps these are some of the other key reasons why our adult lives were so different. Certainly, all the points above help to understand how resilience evolves and differs in children, but our focus here is to understand how Pat missed such an important component of development. Shonkoff (2012) tells us that the following point is a key ingredient in resilience: "The availability of at least one stable, caring, and supportive relationship between a child and an adult caregiver." I had this in abundance, and Pat hardly at all. Why?

As I moved through my education and dual careers as an occupational therapy clinician and professor, I found multiple mentors, colleagues, team leaders, supervisors, friends, teachers, and professors who enabled me to forge "stable, caring and supportive relationships." Early on in my college education, I identified numerous people who I admired and respected. I took advantage of every opportunity to learn from them.

In difficult times, I sought their advice, but perhaps more importantly, I watched and listened as they problem solved. If something was working for them, I wanted to imitate them as I struggled with obstacles. They were my mentors and role models without being formalized.

Pat and I did not share the same view of our brother-in-law Jim. He was a valued resource for me, but not so for Pat. Their relationship was adversarial almost from the beginning. As you read my mom's letters, you will see references to how strained the relationship was between Pat and Jim. The result was that what I saw in Jim was a solid role model whom I interacted with at least three days a week; Pat did not. I also can only think of Dr. Zoll, Mrs. Sauer, and Ma, who could serve as models of resilience and guides in helping Pat develop resilience. However, they were not nearly enough.

Another very related insight from Shonkoff is this pearl: "Resilience depends on supportive, responsive relationships and mastering a set of capabilities that can help us respond and adapt to adversity in healthy ways." He goes on to say, "It's those capacities and relationships that can turn toxic stress into tolerable stress." Pat had far more "adversities" and "toxic stress" than I. He unknowingly desperately needed the acumen he could have absorbed from stable, caring, and supportive adults. Sadly, they may not have been available to Pat, or else he lacked the interpersonal skills to elicit their guidance and wisdom.

Two psychologists, Suzanne C. Kobasa and Salvatore R. Maddi, have done some research and writing on what they call "hardiness." This is very close to reliance, and the definition of hardiness is: "….a group of traits that help people use stressful situations as opportunities to learn and grow. These traits came to be known as the '3 C's: Commitment, Locus of Control (Because LOC was so different with Pat and me, there needs some clarification related to internal And external LOCs. LOC is how much individuals perceive that they themselves have control over

61

their own actions as opposed to events in life occurring because of external forces), and Challenge."

Maddi undertook a 12-year longitudinal study of hardiness in a specific population that resulted in a book, *Hardiness: Turning Stressful Situations Into Resilient Growth* (Maddi, 2013). Kobasa conducted additional research, and together they developed *The Hardiness Test*. This is a self-assessment using multiple-choice options that measure 69 separate variables related to hardiness.

Out of curiosity, I took the Hardiness Test, being as honest as possible on every one of the 200 questions. I then imagined that I was Pat during his best years and took the Hardiness Test again and compared our results. Based on a scale of 1 to 100, Pat's overall hardiness score was 52, and mine was 71, which was not surprising considering how differently we used or did not use mentors and other stable, helpful adults. Also, the trifecta of his burdens (epilepsy, learning disability (AD/HD), and the several (6) ACEs (Adverse Childhood Experiences) he suffered all combined to preclude him from developing a high level of hardiness. His score of 52 was probably attributed to his above-average intelligence (based on my observations of him over 24 years).

Any one of Pat's major burdens would have taken him low and required that he rise and try to move forward. You will see that he did not have all the essential tools and skills of hardiness. Despite these shortcomings, he had some unexpected success.

The Hardiness Test scores result in a summary of strengths and weaknesses. As I did with both ACEs and PACEs scores and findings, I will share both Pat's and my summaries of findings from the Hardiness Test:

Peter:

<u>Strengths:</u>

- Internal locus of control
- High self-esteem
- Very proactive

<u>Potential Strengths:</u>

- Fairly healthy attitude towards problems and challenges
- Fairly resilient
- Reasonably courageous
- Seems to have some sense of purpose
- Relatively perseverant
- Generally willing to take responsibility for your actions or decisions

<u>Challenges/Development Areas:</u>

- Mindset seems to be rather inflexible.
- Very open to new experiences.
- Rather a pessimistic mindset.
- Struggle to find little joys in everyday life.
- Strong sense of self-efficacy.
- Need to nurture adaptability.
- Regulating emotions tends to be a struggle.
- Develop more and healthier coping strategies.

Now, I will compare my Hardiness Test with that of Pat's:

Pat:

<u>Strengths:</u> No strengths detected

Potential Strengths:

- **Tries to find little joys in everyday life**
- **Self-esteem is fairly strong**
- **Reasonably courageous**

Challenges/Development Areas:

- **Rather negative attitude toward problems and challenges.**
- **Level of resilience is not as strong as it could be.**
- **Mindset is rather inflexible.**
- **Not very open to new experiences.**
- **Locus of control is more external than internal.**
- **Mindset is rather pessimistic.**
- **Sense of self-efficacy is not very strong.**
- **Lacks a sense of purpose in life.**
- **Lacks a strong level of perseverance, especially when faced with obstacles.**
- **Need to nurture adaptability.**
- **Tend to be more passive rather than proactive.**
- **Regulating emotions is a struggle.**
- **Accountability appears to be a challenge.**
- **Need to develop more and healthier coping strategies.**

As to be expected, my education and professional experience provided me with more tools that resulted in me having a greater level of hardiness than Pat's. I tried to teach some of these to Pat but to no avail.

I encourage each of you to take the Hardiness Test yourself and then do what I did and take it again using someone you know quite well. To access the Hardiness Test, just Google it and follow the directions. It takes a bit to complete the 200 questions, but you will find the results interesting, I'm sure.

Department were working on Pat, who writhed about, drooling, with his eyes rolled up into his head while a doctor was doing something else. There were also two monks from a nearby Catholic high school who stopped by and seemed to be giving Pat the last rights. Above all, what seemed to be mass hysteria, I could hear Ma crying and pleading. "Please help him. He's dying." I didn't know what to do.

I guess the doctor decided that Pat had to go to the hospital in the ambulance parked out front on the grass. It seemed funny (strange) to put him in the ambulance with the hospital being right across the street, but that is what they did. After the ambulance departed, Ma, Danny, and I made the very short walk across the street and waited in the Emergency Waiting Room to learn what happened to Pat and what they could do to help him. They eventually let us go in to see him, two at a time. He was now conscious but confused about where he was and what had happened to him. We followed Ma's lead and just kept telling him that we were waiting for a specialist to come to see him and what a wonderful specialist he turned out to be.

Dr. John G. Zoll was a neurosurgeon who was called in to evaluate Pat. He was very kind to Pat and clear to all of us in his explanations as to what tests they needed to do in order to find out what had caused Pat to have a grand mal seizure. Little did we know that Dr. Zoll would be the doctor who would take care of Pat for over fifty years until he (Dr. Zoll) retired. Dr. Zoll died on June 15, 2004, at the age of 91. Below is the tribute Pat submitted to the Buffalo News, complete with typos, grammatical errors, and run-on sentences, but it was written right from Pat's heart:

It was good to read that Pat appreciated everything Dr. Zoll did for him over those many years of care, as evinced by the heartfelt message he sent to the family after Dr. Zoll died.

July 27, 2004

dr zoll changed my whole life. He did brain surgery on me back in 1974and I'm a lot better for i owe him my life thank god for him he was a wonderful doctor. i have nothing high regards for him

yours truly

Patrick Talty

Patrick Talty

Pat and Dad, for different reasons, went through a very difficult time in 1956. Dad went through some extensive surgeries on his lungs with no improvement in his breathing. It reached the point where he could no longer work and had to go on Railroad Disability, which reduced his income significantly. He became very depressed, requiring hospitalization and was administered ECT (Electroconvulsive Therapy or what in those days was referred to as "Shock treatments.") After two or three weeks of no progress, his psychiatrist declared that long-term care was the only option, and he was transferred to the Gowanda State Hospital. Since we never owned a car, Ma was dependent on my sister Sue and friends of hers, and Bernie's to take her out to the rural facility that was an hour's treacherous drive away through the middle of what was known as the "Snowbelt."

Here, Ma writes about one of the many trips she and my sister Sue made to the Gowanda State Hospital to visit Dad:

June 18, 1958

Sue & I went to see Dad on Sunday. He looks good and has gained four #. It was a funny but pitiful visit. He has had about seven shock treatments so far, and he didn't remember anything. He didn't know where he was or how long he had been there, nothing about you and Karoline visiting him, Bernard in the service, or Pat being sick.

He told the doctor that morning he was going to report for work. As I said, it was funny, and then again, he was pitiful.

I made that dismal trip to visit Dad several times, and Ma accurately captures the sad reality we usually encountered once we get there. If he was not confused, he was argumentative and hostile toward Ma. His demands were unreasonable in that he wanted Ma to give him more spending money for cigarettes, candy, and outings off-grounds to movies, county fairs, and so forth.

His threatening, cajoling, and whining were all for naught because we were in very dire straits financially at that time. Ma was struggling with the current and growing debt, but two people who could care less were Dad and Pat. Both begged and demanded things Ma could just not afford.

August 14, 1958

We are fine here. Pat stayed home with me this week because Sue wanted a rest from him. (Sue and Ma have been having Pat spend a few days each week at Sue's to give Ma a break.) He is feeling pretty good now, and as I told you before, he is faithful with his pills because he knows now what he has, and he also gets a warning.

He says he hopes he never has any more seizures. Poor little fellow. I feel sorry for him. If it wasn't for that, I would keep him home with me all the time. Danny has been told what to do in case I am at work and anything happens.

Right now, Pat is outside watching the sky for Sputnik III. It was supposed to be visible around 10:43 P.M., and it would be seen in the bowl of the Big Dipper. Ma's love and concern for Pat is quite evident in the above letter. His demanding behavior was wearing Ma down, so my sister Sue let him stay at her house to give Ma a respite, but now Sue needed the respite. Also, the tension between

Ma and Sue over Pat caused a temporary rift in their relationship that greatly saddened Ma.

Ma is trying her best to improve her relationship with my sister, Sue. They used to be more like sisters and best buddies rather than mother and daughter, but they differed greatly on how Pat's outrageous behavior should be managed. This letter is another example of family strife centered on Pat.

August 15, 6:00 A.M.

Sue said to her that Jim & Kathleen were not coming for Sunday dinner anymore after last Sunday. She and I had a set-to (I wonder if Ma knew how appropriate "set-to" was to describe the stressful interactions she and Sue were having over Pat? This definition I found fits very well: "a usually brief and vigorous fight or debate.") *So, she (Sue) said she would send him down to my place on my two days off and on Sundays after church, or if I happen to have Friday & Saturday off, then he will be here for the weekend. Of course, it is all patched up now, but you know how it is kind of shaky ground. She said if things with Pat keep on, we can come visit her in the Gowanda State Hospital. I hope I'll never see that come true.*

Pat has been very good while staying here at home this week. He knows I worry about him while I am working. Practically all week, he has been down to a neighbor's playing. I called his mother and told her that if he wasn't good to send him home. She says that he is being good, and her son doesn't have anyone to play with. That is why when Pat comes down, her son gets outside. Otherwise, he sticks in the house. I remember how well these two lonely kids got along, but they now each had a friend in each other. However, eventually, there must have been something amiss from Pat's perspective because Ma had to push and push to get him to go to his only friend's house or invite him to ours. Strange.

August 22, 1958

The tense and strained relationship between Sue and Ma over Pat is being tested greatly. Here is the latest episode:

Yesterday Sue & I went shopping. Afterward, I went to her house for coffee. She said she was sending Pat back when school started. She says because she can't give the attention to Kathleen (her daughter) that she should give while he is there. I said it was all right with me, but the only thing I worry about is him in the mornings. You see, he has a warning now when these spells come on. He gets a terrific headache and his head shakes. Sue says it is time he was treated like Dan and not like a baby.

So, when school starts, he calls her when he leaves. If she doesn't get a call, she will come down. I don't know how it is going to work, but I didn't tell her. But I wonder what she would say if I said to her when I took care of Kathleen from 6 months to 15 months, if I said that to her, and I had four kids to take care of, too. Oh well, I am not mad because she is nervous, so I am just going to go along. Right now, he is fine and is swimming.

Ma's tolerant and forgiving nature where Pat is the concern is quite apparent here:

August 28, 1958

Ma is very concerned about the unpredictability of Pat's seizures; some are becoming worse:

We are all well here, that is all but Pat. I am not sure, but I think he had another seizure that night. Yesterday and today, he didn't feel too good, and his speech was terrible. He knew what he wanted to say, but no one could understand him. Also, he wet the bed. I have a call in for Dr. Zoll (Pat's neurologist) to try and get to the bottom of the thing. Now, don't get panicky. He is all right; he played outside and rode his bike, but he didn't feel up to par. His appetite is good. But I would like to find out just what is causing these seizures. He is faithful in taking his pills.

September 29, 1958
Dear Tommy & Karoline,

Later, at about 11:00 o'clock this morning, I am going down to Susan's, and together, we are going uptown to the Greyhound depot and taking the bus out to Gowanda to visit Dad. You see, Dad has been allowed home four days a week, but the last two times he was home, he wasn't good at all. In fact, he was just as bad, if not worse, than he was before he went away the first time in March. Not violent, but not eating or talking. He would get all dressed then the next thing I knew, he was back in bed with all his clothes on, even his shoes and covered all up to his neck. So now they have started shock treatments again, which means he can't come home. Susan's car isn't working, and I can't go every week, so he will just have to be satisfied whenever I can get there. Besides, with me on full-time, I don't have every Sunday off either. Was he ever mad because I went on full-time? But maybe it is just as well. As I told him, I've run my legs off since last March, and it hasn't done any good. At least Sue and I haven't seen any improvement.

Pat's birthday went off without a hitch. He had a good time. He has wanted a white shirt like Dan's with the French cuffs. So, I took him out to the Plaza and got him one. Then he bought a model car to put together and some Playdough. I bought him a Pat Boone sweater, three pairs of socks, and a set of cuff links and a tie clip. We had supper then Sue told him he could open his presents. Sue and Jim gave him an Army truck and cannon that connects on the back and shoots plastic cannon balls. Kathleen gave him a dollar.

Ma was carrying quite a load in those days, and it seemed it was now her turn to break down. Not long after Dad went into the State

Hospital, Ma had a major heart attack requiring a month's stay in Mercy Hospital. With Bernie in the Army, Danny, Pat, and I were living alone in the flat. Ma's doctor advised her to stop working because her heart was now so severely damaged that she could die if she overdid it. So, I guess Ma and Sue decided that once again, we would all move back in with Sue and Jim in their little house with just one bathroom.

However, this time, we had two fewer people: Dad was in the Gowanda State Hospital, and his doctors told Ma that "this would probably be his home for the rest of his life." Also, Bernie was now in the Army. So, could two fewer people make combining two families work this time? It was a tentative move at best, but it seems there was no alternative. More toxic stress is coming up, I'm sure.

To help alleviate the inherent problems that can happen when two families occupy the same small living space, Ma and Sue decided that some physical distance in the house could help. Ma's furniture and other stuff would go into the basement, and this would give us a place to go to give Sue and Jim their own family time and space and us, ours.

There was also going to be a greater financial strain that we were about to experience with neither Dad nor Ma working. Indeed, some very stressful times quickly consumed us all. Predictably, Pat wanted things and went quickly into tantrum mode when these were not forthcoming. His unwillingness to try to accept less was beyond reasoning with him. In his distorted thinking, if he was denied anything, he interpreted this as a form of abuse or pummeling and reacted with his usual tantrums.

Chapter 10

The Mental Collapse of Dad

Prior to Dad's psychiatric problems and subsequent admission to the Gowanda State Hospital, we were still living in the trailer. Pat's number one **protective factor** was now a role shared by both Ma and Dad. However, Dad's declining health precluded him from actively continuing in this role. He no longer had the necessary energy or resolve to maintain this role. Pat's academic and interpersonal struggles became less of an issue with Dad's declining ability to function. Unfortunately, Dad was still a two-pack-a-day smoker throughout his adult life, and he was recently diagnosed with severe emphysema, which is a form of COPD. We really didn't know how sick he was. He continued to work full-time and smoke because, back in the 1950s, it was not well publicized how lethal smoking was.

Due to his shortness of breath, chest pain, and bouts of coughing, he had to reduce his housework activities and getting to and from work was becoming increasingly difficult. Walking had become very hard for him. Even walking the quarter mile from our trailer to the bus stop and walking into the steel plant where he ran a diesel locomotive was becoming near impossible. His demeanor also changed as he struggled to carry on with his normal activities. He was very irritable, frustrated, and intolerant of all of us, even Pat. Because we did not know the gravity of his progressive disease, we did not adjust our expectations. We also did not improve our behavior or our schoolwork. We were bad. Also, Pat's usual manipulations of Dad were now unsuccessful, which confused and aggravated Pat. Dad now ignored Pat or vented his repressed anger at Pat because he was an available target to pummel.

When Dad was no longer able to work, we experienced another family catastrophe and, of course, another form of an ACE. Ma and Dad had to sell our beloved trailer and move us into a flat back in our old neighborhood. We were all very sad about leaving the trailer camp lifestyle behind. In this Pat and I were in concert. However, this move would bring us geographically closer to our sister, Sue. She was always a big help to us, but the three-mile drive from her home to the trailer camp had become a large barrier. We would now be less than a mile away.

So, Dad's three years of emerging success as a Dad, husband, homeowner, and neighbor were over because his physical illness now dominated his life. However, he did try to continue as a railroad engineer as long as possible. His earnings, combined with Ma's pay from her full-time job in Central Supply at the local hospital, enabled us to live comfortably in the trailer, but when Dad could not work, another calamity would challenge our family greatly.

Pat quitting High School removed one large source of the pummeling that emanated from his fellow students and teachers but exposed him to the repeated rejections (pummelings) from the potential employers of the many low-level jobs he sought. Ma suggested that he return to school, but he wouldn't hear of it, which is understandable considering his poor history in the classroom. Dad offered neither advice nor support. He was consumed with himself and his rapidly declining health.

Moving in with Sue and Jim again generated new problems and made familiar problems worse. Having Dad placed in the State Hospital due to the deterioration of his mental health eased some of the day-to-day stress for Ma and Sue, but Pat's acting out and Dad's demanding behavior from afar made life very difficult for us all.

The following excerpt from one of Ma's letters shows Dad's declining function and the related strain on Ma's and Sue's fraying relationship.

October 4, 1958

Now about Dad. From the first of September, they had been letting him come home four days a week. He still bitched about being out there. I told him he should consider himself lucky, only having to be out there for three days. He would run me ragged to the drug store to get his prescription bottles filled and smoke every cigarette. He still had thoughts of doing away with himself and everyone else. On the days I had to work 3-11, he never talked to the boys or cared if they stayed out all night. He just stayed in bed or on the davenport all day long. So, when we took him back on a Sunday night, I made up my mind to tell the doctor. So, the next day, I was off, and I called the doctor and told him everything. I tried to put my arms around him (Dad) and tell him we needed him, but he just simply ignored me. After I got through telling the doctor, he said I needn't worry because he wouldn't be coming home for quite a while. He said, I (me) must work, and the children have to go to school, and none of that can be accomplished without proper rest. So now they have started electric shock treatments again. Last Tuesday, I was off, and Sue and I went out on the bus. He was pretty good and wanted me to bring him home, but I said I couldn't afford to. If he wanted to go home on the bus, I would have to stay and that was out. He laughed. I can't go out tomorrow because I am working, but I will go out on Tuesday on the bus.

Sue and Jim couldn't afford to have the car fixed. It would have cost them $150, as much as they paid for the car. So, they turned it in on another car. I think she said it was a 1953 four-dour door Ford. So, I am going to get my permit and drive, too.

Because Ma was so consumed with Dad and Pat this put a great strain on her relationship with my sister Sue. Poor Sue. What a toll! She must have been overwhelmed with all of us descending on her and her young family once again. Think of all that strain we brought with us, like Dad and Pat and all that came with them. Toxic stress at its worst. She was a very strong and capable woman, but I still, to this day, am in awe of what she took on. In retrospect, I doubt we ever thanked her for all that she did trying to help us. It was a horrendous load, with Dad and Pat being big parts of it. Ma gives us a glimpse of how Dad's behavior impacted the family (this event took place just a few days after she was discharged from the hospital after spending four weeks there following her most recent heart attack):

November 25, 21958

*Monday night, while we were all eating supper, the telephone rang. It was Tom (*Dad*). He said the doctor told him he could come home for a whole week. Sue said that was an impossibility because I was still in bed, and we couldn't have him up all night prowling around the house. She also told him it wouldn't be any good for me or Pat. Of course, I went all to pieces because I just dreaded subjecting the children to his silly ways.*

So, Sue told him a couple of days, but not for a week. Of course, he was mad. Yesterday morning, we dreaded calling the doctor in Gowanda. He said he never said such a thing, that with the situation at home, me sick, that he would suggest one day but not overnight. Now, Sue has just come home from shopping ($40), and as soon as Kathleen eats her dinner, she goes out to Gowanda, takes him clean clothes and gives him the bus fare to come in tomorrow. Then, she and Jim will take him back tomorrow night. I just know he is going to be mad, but there is nothing else that can be done.

The only thing that can be said is that they (Gowanda) doctors are very lax with those patients. But just as the doctor told me, sometimes the patients get carried away with themselves when they are told they can go home for a day. I hope Sue doesn't have any trouble with him. How I wish I could go with her, but I know the long ride wouldn't do me any good. I just took a bath and that just about pooped me out. In these times of great tension, it did not take much to generate great angst in all present. Pat's seizures became more unpredictable, more severe, and more disruptive to anything that was going on when a seizure would commence. They generated chaos, and when they were over, he went into a deep sleep. Here is an example of one of Pat's particularly severe seizures, as described in a letter from Ma:

December 2, 1958

Friday morning, Patrick woke up with a terrible headache. I gave him a pill, but by nine-thirty, he was in a seizure. Jim and Sue rushed him to the hospital. Sue drove up Abbott Road at about 70 miles an hour with her hand on the horn. Jim sat in the back seat, holding Pat in his arms. They only kept him for about 3 hours because the hospital was so crowded. He came out of it OK, but he stayed in bed practically all day here at home. Sue and I were so nervous, so she and I baked eight loaves of bread. Saturday, Pat went to Seneca Street to do his Christmas shopping. When he came home, he didn't feel good, and he told me he had two sick spells on Seneca Street and wet himself. You see, he loses control of his bladder when he has seizures. I am thinking seriously of having a piece of paper for him to always carry with him with his name, address, telephone number and a notice that says, "I am an epileptic." What do you think? Of course, he didn't have a seizure on Seneca Street, only a sick spell.

When Pat woke up after a seizure, he was always irritable and lethargic. It annoyed Sue that Ma catered to Pat's every wish and demand despite his attitude of rejection of her help and suggestions. Each seizure proved traumatic for everyone present except, of course, Dad. It seems that Dad was so worried about his shortness of breath, his fear of a heart attack, and his pure hatred of having to be incarcerated in a State Mental Hospital that Pat's seizures did not impact him a bit. I think this shows how his priorities have so severely shifted. It was another form of pummeling for Pat, with Dad appearing unconcerned about Pat's seizures. Was this also another ACE for Pat? If not an additional ACE, it was at least reinforcing an existing ACE.

Chapter 11

Pat's ACEs at Twelve Years of Age: 1959

Below are Ma's worries and stressors to date, and whatever stresses Ma experienced surely impacted the environment Pat was living in and, of course, Pat himself:

- Dad's discharge from the Gowanda State Hospital is now imminent, but his mental stability is still a great concern for us all.

- Sue strongly encouraged Ma not to return to Dad because of the pain he has brought us all and told Ma if we go, she is done rescuing us. (Ma, of course, was conflicted).

- There also was the inevitable tension that is common when two families occupy the same home.

- Ma missed Tommy and Karoline terribly but found great solace in expressing her thoughts, feelings, and dreams by writing letters to them.

- There is also the present financial burden, especially for Sue and Jim, making it necessary for Jim to take a second job and for Sue to start looking for a job herself.

- The future financial picture is still uncertain in terms of what Dad's Disability pension will amount to and whether it will be sufficient to support us all.

- Ma's health (heart condition) is still not resolved and may prevent her from ever returning to work.

- Pat's epilepsy continues to be a problem with frequent "sick spells" and seizures, often without warning.

The spring of 1959 school environment seemed to be one of Pat's better times. He was in the fifth grade and had a very supportive teacher. Ma was pleased to include some good news about Pat in her letters during this time. Before we get to Ma's excerpts, let's hear from Pat in his letter to Tommy and Karoline around the same time:

115 Kimmel

Buffalo 20, N.Y

March 4, 1959

Dear Tommy & Karoline,

I am fine and so is everybody else. I got a transistor radio. And it's got an earphone on it. I can carry it in my pocket. And it works well. It is as big as a cigarette pack. I can get 6 stations on it. I heard Karoline's mother can get up now. I am having a good time in school too. My teacher's name is Mrs. Sauer. Peter had her in fifth grade too. I heard you hung my picture of Donald Duck on the wall. Well, I'm going to leave you now. So long.

Your brother

Pat

PS Don't forget to write me a letter.

Love,

Little Shaver (Ma's nickname for Pat)

His letter is very positive and shows quite an improvement in his writing abilities. It is also significant that he does not once mention his seizures. Does this mean his seizures are no longer an ACE? Not likely.

Now, Ma's excerpts related to Pat's school environment:

March 6, 1959

Patrick was on the stage today, too. He was the announcer for some kind of program they were having at school today. He had to say: "Good Afternoon, School #72 welcomes all of you. Now, would everyone please stand, salute the flag, and sing one verse of our National Anthem." At the close of the program, he had to say: "I hope all of you enjoyed the program. Thank you one and all. See you later."

April 16th, 1959

*I told you that Patrick belongs to the Boy Scouts (*another positive environment!*) down here at St. Agatha's, didn't I? Well, the mothers of the scouts formed a club to help buy things they don't have and help some boys who don't have enough money for camp. Tonight, they are meeting to elect officers. Then, one night a month, we will meet. Right now, we are raffling off an Infant of Prague. Each book of tickets a boy scout sells is worth $1.00, and that money goes toward his camp money.*

April 18, 1959

I went to that Boy Scout meeting and your mother was elected President. Wowee!! I will also tell you about those tickets. Well, Pat already has sold 5 books and has the $5 credited to his name toward him going to camp. He already knows that he can't go this year, but next year he will. It costs about $40 alone, without spending money and the different things he will need. The Scout Master says he is really trying. Thursday night, he passed two tests: First Aid and Camping Methods. He has a few more tests to take then he will be a second-class scout.

April 29, 1959

A mixture of good and not-so-good grades: *Pat just came home with his spelling paper. He had 7 wrong. He isn't too good in spelling, but he makes up for it in Math. In spelling, I want to give you an example: honest = unrest, exercise = extrasize. It looks to me like he spells the way the word sounds to him.* These errors could be attributed to AD/HD, but without a formal evaluation, this is just a hypothesis on my part.

May 8, 1959

Tonight, Pat and I were all alone. Sue & Kathleen went visiting to Eleanor Griffin's. She just had a new baby. Jim was working, Peter went out, and Dan went to the show. Pat & I had a television party. (A "television party" was a family thing that consisted of just potato chips and soda pop). Pat loved them and would have been very happy with just him and Ma to share the experience and the potato chips.

May 12, 1959

Patrick is doing very well. Here are his marks: Reading 84, Spelling 90, Arithmetic 85, Geography 83, English 81, History 84, Science 85, Penmanship C (80-89), and Hygiene 84. His average was 92. He went up in everything by one point except English, where he went down one point. I am so glad that he is doing good. His teacher says he is trying very hard. He becomes very dizzy and nauseated. So, I guess I will call Dr. Zoll and make an appointment for him to see Pat and check him over. Perhaps he does not have AD/HD? It's possible, but I doubt it.

August 13, 1959

Right now, Sue & Jim are having marital troubles. Jim is going to leave after the baby is born (Sue is pregnant) in December or January. He says he wants to be alone. I have asked Sue if we are the cause, but she said she asked Jim, but he said no, but you know he wouldn't say anything to hurt me or the boys. But you can see yourself Sue, Jim and Kathleen never have a minute to themselves. There is always some of us around. Sue says if he does leave in January, she will get a legal separation. I hate to see that happen.

Peter knows the score, and he wants to quit school and work for Bern full-time so we can go for ourselves. Peter has grown up overnight. I am going to buy a car so that I can get out more with Pat and Dan.

Peter is saving his money to help defray the expenses of his insurance on the car. I really think he is going to be my backbone along with you. He has gotten very disgusted with school because he failed, and next June, he will not graduate along with his friends.

If I go housekeeping, I will have to get Bernard out of the Army on a Hardship, which I think he will like, because he does not care for Army life, and he still has about 17 months left to serve. If I do that, what procedures do I have to go through? I mean getting him out on a Hardship.

Tommy & Karoline, I knew it was going to come to this; I could see the handwriting on the wall when Jim asked me to move in here. But at the time, there wasn't anything else I could do. Believe me, I sure appreciated and was thankful. I had a place to go and knew the boys were taken care of. Peter said he wants me to quit my job if we go.

Sue says she really thinks it would be best and she hopes I don't think she is putting me out. I told her I don't think that way at all, but right now, her happiness is all that I want, and I think the quicker we go, the quicker things will straighten themselves out.

When we all moved in with Sue and Jim five years ago, it was Sue who was the initiator of the need for us to move out that really worked out well for everyone. Dad got sober, and we had our own home, even if it was only a trailer. Dad was able to get us out of debt, and Sue and Jim could have their home and life back. This time, it was different because it was Ma who decided that we had to go and go we did. Due to Ma's resourcefulness, within a month, we were moved into a flat on the fringe of our favorite neighborhood of South Buffalo. It is known colloquially as "Kaiser-Town."

I need to expand Pat's environment to include the Gowanda State Hospital, where Dad has been for the past three years. Below is an excerpt from Ma describing a recent visit she and Pat had with Dad:

October 9, 1959

Pat and I went out to Gowanda. Dad was sitting watching the World Series. When he saw us, he came over, never asked Pat or me how we were, just when I was going to get him out of there. The same old questions. I told him I wanted to see the doctor. He said what for and what have you got to say to him that is of any interest to him? I talked to the doctor anyway and he said that he doubts if Dad would ever be able to come home, and it is out of the question to even consider him living alone, so the next best thing to do is to make him a ward of the state of New York.

I said but would the state release him if I got a place of my own and the doctor said no, but I could take him home occasionally, providing they make him a ward. Who is going to tell him that? Yesterday, he was positively terrible; he ranted and raved at me the whole time I was there. He said if I didn't fight a little bit for him, he was going to commit suicide, and if he did that for me or not, he did not want any of the family to cry over him because it is all my fault. He hates every one of us. You should have heard him. It was

85

awful. Imagine the impact this visit had on Pat. Read the next excerpt.

Poor Pat, he was so worried about me for fear I was going to have a heart attack. I really believe if I did have one out there, he (Pat) would have killed his father. Dad said, You think you are so important with your G _ _ d _ _ car while I rot out here, locked up." *I said, "Well, Tom, I was locked up for 30 years and now look at me." I thought he was going to strangle me. He also said he was going to catch the 5:15 bus to Buffalo, get his winter coat that's there and his clothes, go uptown, get drunk, and if anyone came near him to take him back to Gowanda, he would knife them, including me." Can you blame me for not wanting to go out there anymore? If I took him out of there, he would spend the rest of his life telling me what I did to him.*

This was a most stressful visit for both Ma and Pat and perhaps even more so for Dad. It clearly describes someone (Dad) who is not ready to be discharged home, which was a relief to us all. It most definitely would qualify as another ACE for Pat.

There are some self-disclosures about my role in causing further strife for Ma and indirectly for Pat that chronologically fit here. For reasons that only a seasoned counselor or psychiatrist can explain, but in short, I went crazy! Over a six-month period, I quit high school, stole cars, got fired from the gas station that my brother-in-law Jim owned, broke into homes and businesses, wrecked Ma's beloved car, and was planning an armed robbery when I was arrested. Imagine Ma receiving this terrible news during everything else that is cascading on her. Still, to this day, I feel terrible for this crazy era of my life, but I feel good that Ma lived long enough to see me turn my life around and achieve a high degree of family and professional success.

As part of my crazy stage, I took great pleasure in pummeling Pat. It had a physical element because we both liked to wrestle, but I was better at it, causing him to become enraged and this I knew. So, here is Ma's description of the consequences of one of my pummelings when I was crazy and bored:

November 6, 1959

Can you imagine the last day (Monday) that I worked, I got 3 phone calls from Pat. I guess the two of them (he and Peter) raised hell, and I sure did over the phone. Finally, in the end, I had Peter take him out to the hospital at about 9:30. Pat deliberately took the light off Danny's bed and smashed it on the floor. I think that kid could use some shock treatment. Like I said, I was crazy, so I pummeled Pat and made him crazy. I was out of control.

Chapter 12

Ma's Stressors of 1960 that Greatly Impacted Pat

- Dad's discharge to home on Christmas Eve with little notice.
- Ongoing financial struggles.
- My arrest, upcoming hearing and sentencing, and my overall awful behavior.
- Pat's epilepsy and bizarre behavior.
- Ma's heart condition.
- Me demolishing Ma's beloved car.
- The sudden presence in her life of Wasson Ma's long-absent brother.
- Sue and Jim's struggles.

Ma offers further proof that I really was crazy back then, and I do not deny it: My arrest, felony conviction, fines, legal fees, and 18 months on Probation enabled me to turn my life around. Fortunately, this all happened before I turned 18, and so my record was sealed, and I was granted Youthful Offender status. I only share this because it shows in Ma's letters.

Patrick has been sick since last Friday. He hasn't been to school all week. I hate to leave him to go to work, but he is pretty good about it. I guess by the lady upstairs, they really do raise holy hell. She has called them more than once. It isn't so much Pat & Dan, it is Peter. Sue and I were talking, and she and I both said he (Peter) could use some psychotherapy or something. If I told you some of the things he does, I'm sure you would agree. Last Sunday, he had to open the gas station. He asked Dan to go with him. At about 10:30 A.M., he decided to close the gas station and go for some coffee. Jim has a jeep with no license plates on it. They are going to use it to plow and tow. He beat Danny up because Dan wouldn't drive it. Imagine he took it? If he had been stopped, Jim would have lost the gas station. For that, they just about hang you here. He also made Dan pump gas. The fellow across the street reported to the police that a kid about 13 or 14 was pumping gas. So, the police came to the garage when Jim was there. Jimmy, of course, denied it. He (Peter) has been staying out all night. So, the other day, I told him he must start coming in at a decent hour, or I am going to be arrested as a wayward minor.

January 8, 1960

It is surprising that at the age of 14, Pat continues to be so egocentric as his following behavior described by Ma certainly attests to:

Pat is awfully jealous of Shawn (Sue's baby). While I was holding him, Pat wouldn't even come out of the bedroom. Bernard took Shawn home, I was down in the cellar, finishing up the wash, and Pat came down. He knocked me off my feet (literally speaking) when he said, "Why do you have to act so silly about that baby?" How do you like that? He also says next Christmas, he isn't going over to Susan's at all because between Kathleen and Shawn, no one will be able to get into the living room with all the toys and stuff they will get. I just let those things go over my head. If I tried to explain, he wouldn't listen anyway. When I did get through explaining, he would still say and act the same way.

Pat's behavior in relation to Sue's new baby was bewildering to us all.

January 21, 1960

Dad was discharged from the Gowanda State Hospital on Christmas Eve, and Ma is feeling pretty good about having him home:

It seems good to have Dad home because he keeps peace here while I am working. At least I don't get 6 or 7 phone calls at work. He is pretty good mentally, but physically, he is not good. He does breakfast dishes and makes the beds. That is a big help. He says he has been sleeping better since he came home. He even does the cooking while I am working.

For the first time in over three years, we were all together under one roof. Bernie was out of the Army and Dad was discharged from the Gowanda State Hospital. The good feeling was short-lived because, within a year, Danny had quit high school and enlisted in the Navy.

The flat Ma found for us was nice, but it was not in our old neighborhood of South Buffalo, and that is where our friends all lived. The other problem with it was the distance to Sue's house was a problem. She did not have a working car and the bus connections were inconvenient. Lastly, we had a very controlling landlord whose daughter lived upstairs and reported all the things she found annoying about us to her father. With each "infraction," he was ringing our doorbell. Dad had nicknamed him "Khrushchev" because of his dictatorial ways. In any event, Ma found us a flat in South Buffalo that met all our requirements, plus the one she wanted in being close to Seneca Street with all the places where she and Sue could meet and shop together,

Chapter 13

Taking Stock: Pat

Each paragraph below is an evolving ACE (Adverse Childhood Experiences or traumatic events that Pat experienced before the age of 18, and are the precursors of negative health and behavior outcomes in his later life):

Pat was not the only lost sheep that Ma worried about and tried to corral for our own protection. Yes, my many indiscretions when I was 17 were a great burden to Ma, as were Danny's. My being arrested turned out to be the best thing to happen to me, and we all hoped that joining the Navy would have the same maturing effect on him. But what about Pat, who is really the focus of this book?

In terms of school environments, Pat was expected to adjust to eight different grammar schools and eight different neighborhoods over a ten-year period. He did not do well in terms of adapting to these significant changes as a kid. He essentially remained friendless, but most critically, his seizures could not be eradicated. His seizure disorder was his plague throughout his life. He missed several days of school due to his "sick spells," which may have been harbingers of grand mal seizures to follow.

Happiness was rare for Pat. It seemed he spent much of his waking hours wishing he could be seizure-free, have friends, have the respect of his peers and teachers, and have all the toys he saw on TV or neighborhood kids enjoying. He was very envious of their cars, their vacations, their homes, their bikes, their clothes, and so forth.

His inadequacies served as the fuel for ridicule, mocking, derision, and rejection, or in other words, pummeling from his peers.

It was at home that Pat was impacted by the heavy and sad burdens that Ma carried. She has had several heart attacks, some necessitating lengthy periods of hospitalization. He was terrified that Ma may die, as we all were. However, I think he thought if Ma were to die, he would lose the only person who really loved him. We all loved and worried about Pat, but we did not show this to him in overt ways.

Pat was conflicted about Dad. When Dad's physical and mental health deteriorated, and he no longer could be Pat's protector and "aide-de-camp," Pat was confused. Then, when Dad was hospitalized in the State Hospital, Pat saw first-hand how demanding Dad was of Ma. Her stress becoming his stress, but he was incapable of protecting her from Dad's hostility and criticism. All he could do was beg Ma not to let Dad come home.

Pat became insanely jealous of Sue's daughter Kathleen and now her son Shawn was beyond explanation. When he threatened Kathleen with bodily harm, Ma knew we had to move out of Sue and Jim's house before something terrible happened.

With our moving out, Ma and Sue were able to reconcile and enjoy each other's company once again. Did this reconciliation include Pat? Sue tolerated him but could not get past the devastation he caused in her home with his hostile focus on her daughter Kathleen.

Chapter 14

"Kaisertown"

At 14 years of age, Pat was not well-equipped to manage life in a new neighborhood, a different culture from Irish to Polish, and a new school. He showed that he had a sharp mind, but it was enmeshed in the social and neurological malfunctions that characterized his daily life. He carried with him the seizure disorder, his ACEs, his AD/HD learning disabilities, and the limited protective factors available to him.

Ma was pleased that she found us "a nice flat," but it was not in our familiar neighborhood of South Buffalo, which Danny, Pat, and I all resented. But we were in our own place and Susan and Jim could work on getting back together. There were however some "issues" in our Kaisertown flat that Ma shared with Tommy and Karoline.

Another positive thing about our new flat is that Dad was discharged from the psychiatric hospital, and it felt good to have him back home with us. His mood was better, and his biggest problem was his difficulty breathing. Bernie was also able to join us because he received a Hardship discharge from the Army. We all liked being back together again.

May 1, 1960

We are all well here, but the woman upstairs is a terror. Her father owns the house, and he lives in Cheektowaga. She was leaving notes on the back door for me until I got fed up and called her father. He came over and apologized to me and for her and said there will be no more notes. Now she started again. So, I blew my top at her. She said she was going to call her father to have me put out. I told her to go ahead, but first, I had a few things to say. Well, anyway, it didn't help me to feel better, and I just simply ignored the whole thing. She didn't call her father because she knew she wouldn't get very far.

For some reason, we had a history of not doing well with landlords and landladies. This may have been because we do get loud and are not rigid followers of rules. Also, if we don't like the rules, we just ignore them. I would not like to rent to us.

Also, on May 1, 1960:

Yesterday, while Dad and I were doing the windows, Pat came into the yard, dripping blood from his mouth. He had cut his tongue. Don't ask me how he did it. I can't understand it yet. Anyway, he cried and yelled like Pat does. You know. I stopped the bleeding and took him over to the Mercy Hospital for a tetanus shot. They didn't give him any shot because he had one last summer, but the doctor said to keep him on soft foods for 3 days. Right away, I took out the pocketbook because he was already headed for the cafeteria for a milkshake. What a guy!

June 11, 1960

Below is Ma's detailed account of her recent heart attack, necessitating a six-week stay in the same hospital where she worked full-time. She loves it there because all her co-workers stop to see her. Dad is struggling with his breathing, and Ma is very worried about him. Ma and Dad's declining health is impacting Pat greatly (an ACE in the making).

Did I tell you about it (my attack)? Well, the day before (the 8th of May), I helped Danny. He painted my porch. When he finished, I did all the trim (around the windows and doors). While he was painting, I washed and hung clothes out. After the clothes were dry and he had finished the second layer, I took all the clothes down, folded them, put them away, and got my pail of water. I scrubbed all the woodwork, washed the windows, ironed the drapes, hung them and scrubbed the floor. Danny and Pat put the furniture back in place. I took a bath and relaxed all evening after supper.

The next day (Sunday), I ate, made the beds, Dad did the dishes, washed my hair, and set it and Wasson (Ma's brother), Dan, and I were sitting at the kitchen table, trying to teach Dan to play pinochle. Sue had called to ask me if I would take care of Shawn. She and Kathleen wanted to go to Albion to Santa Claus Land. So, I was waiting for her to come over. Dad had said he wanted to read the Sunday paper, and then he would play, too. So, there we were. Dan, Wasson, and I had played about 5 games with cards turned up and Dad came out. He said he would "kibitz" for Dan and show him how to hold his cards. I looked over at Dad and everything started to spin, and I said, "Oh my God, what's the matter? I can't see anything." The next thing I remember was the Rescue Squad was giving me oxygen. Sue said I didn't fall off the chair because Dan and Dad were holding me. She said when she stopped the car out front of the house, she could hear me gasping for breath out there. She called the Rescue Squad, and they didn't get there right away (6 minutes), so Bernard got in the car and drove over. He just got there, and the Rescue Squad was pulling out. When I came to, all you could see were policemen, firemen, and doctors because when the Rescue Squad saw me, they called the Mercy Hospital ambulance. Later, the doctors carried me on the chair back to the bed. I got the "shakes" and couldn't even talk, so one of the doctors called Dr. Sullivan.

They had asked me if I wanted to go to the hospital and I told them no, but when he called Dr. Sullivan, he didn't ask; he told me I would be admitted. "No" is one thing you don't say to him. It seems like a bad dream now, but it sure was horrible while it lasted. Yesterday, Dad came over to see me. He said I should know now that it is true love for him to come out in 90-degree temperature. Sue said, "Love, hell, you just wanted to get her out of the house." He looks terrible, and he only weighs 95 pounds. Today, he is going to the doctor for his usual checkup. I am hoping he will put him in the hospital just to build him up.

Below is some good news about Pat and how much he helps Dad: Ma also describes what could be evidence of his maturing and perhaps becoming a bit less egocentric, which would be good.

June 19, 1960

Today, Sue took Patrick to the ear, nose, & throat doctor. Remember the time he broke his nose in Texas? Well, now he is having a hard time breathing on the one side. If he goes swimming, the one side he can't breathe through swells up. The doctor told Sue that he doesn't want to do anything to the nose until he is about 17 years old. So, he gave him a prescription for some medication and a spray. He wants to see Pat a week from today. If this spray doesn't help, I don't know what he will do. Even before the swimming season started, he would complain about his nose, and it is so out of shape. He's so glad to have me home. Sunday night, I took a walk over to the store. It is just 2 doors away. He was standing out in front of the store with the people that run the store. He saw me coming and he said, "Here comes my mother. Isn't she a beautiful sight?" He has sympathy for a person and understanding. He has been a big help to Dad. He has done the shopping, scrubbing, and waxing. Now he is going to clean for me. All he wants me to do is sit and supervise. He gets Dad a little excited now and then, but he and Peter have helped financially and mentally.

The saga of Pat's seizures goes on and on, as does Ma's concern and care for him. This next vignette shows all of this despite Ma's somewhat fragile state due to her history of heart problems and limitations that she ignores when she is needed.

Pat had one of the happiest days of his life, as described in the excerpt below, but I think it was sad that he had no one to share this big event with:

August 14, 1960

Yesterday the Hamburg Fair started. I wanted to take Pat, but I was afraid because of the heat and the crowd. No place to sit except in buildings and he doesn't like that. So, today, Dad and I decided to let him go himself. I called the bus company and got the price. I gave him $10 and bus fare and extra bus fare in case he lost some. He was so happy he was almost crying. Pat always loved the Hamburg Fair!

Is Pat maturing? The next excerpt suggests not, but the last part suggests he could be. Regardless, he created another stressful event for Ma to handle.

August 25, 1960

I had to punish Pat yesterday. The night before last, we were watching television and Bernard was sleeping. Peter had gone to bed and Danny was out with his friends. Pat was sitting out in front of the store (2 doors from us), visiting with the people. His bike was parked on the side. Danny came along and made believe he was going to take the bike. Pat ran home here, got his lock and Danny's

97

lock, went back, and put the two locks on his bike. Danny told him to give him back his lock, or he would punch him. Pat said no, that the locks were going to stay on. So, then Pat started to kick Dan. He kicked him once in the rear and when Dan turned around, he (Pat) told Dan he would kick him where he wouldn't be able to walk and Dan grabbed his leg, and Pat fell on the sidewalk. He screamed so terrible that I could hear him above the television; the neighbors were all out because he had wakened up two babies. I ran out and Pat got up and ran the other way. I told him it wasn't the fighting I was punishing him for. It was the awful screaming.

He just woke up and asked me if he could have his bike. I told him yes, but first, he had to go to the A&P and do some shopping for me. He is very good at shopping. Dad sent Dan once while I was in the hospital, and he came home with only half of what was on the list, whereas Pat takes his time and looks around until he finds what he wants.

The following excerpt was written by my sister Sue for reasons she makes very clear:

September 15

I am writing this letter for Mother. She is back in the hospital. She had a very bad heart attack at 5:00 A.M. Saturday. She has been in an oxygen tent up until yesterday. She is not allowed to write or even feed herself. I will be doing the writing for her, but you can address the letters to her in the hospital. Please notice it is <u>Mercy.</u> *We could not make it to the Victory* (Our Lady of Victory Hospital, where Ma was usually admitted) *this time.*

As 1960 was ending, both Ma's and Dad's health were in serious decline. Dad's emphysema had progressed to the point where he could not do physical work like housework without getting out of

98

breath. He was suffering terribly. In addition, his mental health has also declined, requiring him to take three tranquilizers every day. Ma has had numerous heart attacks, with each resulting in several weeks of hospitalization. Her doctor continues to recommend that she stop working strongly, but she staunchly refuses. During her most recent hospitalization, she was also diagnosed with diabetes. Unfortunately, my three brothers and I didn't appreciate how sick Ma and Dad were. We just went on with our lives, leaving all the housework for Dad, who struggled greatly. Looking back, our parents' physical decline was obvious, but not to us boys. Typically, we were focused on ourselves and our own lives.

Ma showed her frustration with Danny and Pat when their report cards came out:

November 4, 1960

Danny brought home his Report Card. He passed one subject out of five. Pat failed everything. These two are just hopeless and helpless. It is so unusual to hear Ma use such harsh and almost condemning language in talking about Danny and Pat. It may have been related to her repeated heart attacks and she just did not have it in her to be optimistic. This unusual negative and hopeless perspective appears again in one of her later letters below.

:

November 19, 1960

Pat is still the same old Pat. He is so fat; he weighs as much as Sue, if not more, and she weighs 150 pounds. Pat and Dad don't get along at all, especially if I am home, because Pat likes me to think Dad is always picking on him, which I know isn't so. His schoolwork isn't good either. He hasn't had any more seizures, thank goodness, but he does have some terrific sick spells. I took him to his doctor, but he said Pat doesn't need any medication. He has had some bad spells in school, so they let him lie down on a couch in the Nurse's office until he feels better, or if he is too bad, they bring him home.

February 2, 1961

Why do you say you are the only one spoiled? I spoiled every one of you kids. But of all of them, I think Pat is the worst. On February 10th, I have an appointment for Pat to be (I don't know how to spell it), but it sounds like psychoanalyzed. It is being done through the Catholic Charities on the recommendation of School #69, where he goes. The child (Pat) is terribly nervous, and he has been giving the teachers a bad time because he doesn't know the work. As far as me with him, he is so afraid something is going to happen to me, and he says no one wants him but me. He hangs onto me terribly because he is afraid I will go back to the hospital and, this time, die. He takes care of me and won't let me do anything if he is around. As I say, he is good to me, but then, on the other hand, he argues with everyone, then turns to me and says, "Don't worry, Mother, just don't pay any attention to them." I will let you know the outcome of our session. I said, one day, between him and Dad, they tore me to pieces.

The above is a classic description of a kid with AD/HD. Ma is probably going to an agency for some sort of psychological assessment. I assume the results will not reflect the current thinking of developmental specialists because the classification of AD/HD was still not known back in 1961. The truth is we, the professionals, were all ignorant about AD/HD. I was in OT school at the University at Buffalo, taking a course centered on normal neuroanatomy and neurophysiology and a subsequent course in neuropathology, where we studied a wide range of neurological

The stress level in our home currently is palpable, but now it is not due to Ma and Dad's disabling health conditions. The focus is on Pat's imminent school torment: Final Exams! Here is Ma's description of the pending disaster:

June 15 and 16, 1961

Tomorrow, examinations for public grammar and high schools start. Pat went to bed at about eight o'clock. He has himself so worked up, what with crying and worrying for fear he won't pass. I'm afraid he might be sick and won't be able to go to school.

Well, Pat was OK this morning. At least he went to school. When I heard him crying last night, I sort of suspected what was the matter. So, I went to him and sat on the side of the bed and talked to him. He kind of quieted down after that and fell off to sleep. I thought he would be sick or have a seizure this morning.

Pat's performance on the exams was worse than we could have anticipated. See Ma's unusually sardonic view below:

June 30, 1961

Pat failed everything with 20's and 30's, but he is getting so big and fat that they put him in 8th grade "On Condition." He felt better, but as I told him, he must work twice as hard this year because he can't go into high school "On Condition." He said well, Tommy will help me and he sure can use it.

It is sad to read that Pat is relieved to be moving on to eighth grade "On Condition." The "On Condition" is a path Danny and I, and of course Pat, are very familiar with. Each year, it was the common way for the three of us to move through Grammar school. I can understand why he felt better. We never "got sent back." no matter how poorly we did in the next grade. It was an empty threat, and we knew this from lots of experience.

In Ma's letter below, she describes another tragedy for Pat that has the potential to be an element of another ACE. By itself, it would not be an ACE, but coupled with other future losses before he reaches 19 years old, another ACE could be the result:

August 7, 1961

Pat had his beautiful Schwinn bike stolen yesterday. He had it chained to the bike frame over at the park with a Policeman sitting right there. They sawed through the chain. Today, I bet he will be sick. We reported it, but so far, nothing. This is the third time it has been stolen in less than a year. I bought it for his birthday last year. It cost $72. He was so proud of his new bike and rode it all over. He was, of course, devastated, *as were we.*

Note: The above was the last letter from Ma in 1961. Tommy had returned home to the States in August and was then stationed in Rome, New York, but we have no letters from Ma from August of 1961 to January of 1962. Apparently, they communicated in person and by telephone during this time. However, Ma states in her letter below that she misses writing her letters and thus returned to writing them.

January 8, 1962, Ma resumed her letter writing on this date and put together a scenario that depicts how tragic and sad Pat's life has become:

Poor Pat. I know he is a disturbed child, but just the same, I feel bad for him. Last night, he went to church at 7. At that time, he was OK. But earlier in the afternoon, he went berserk with his model train. He took it off the board, packed it all away and swore and cursed at all of us. He said some night he was going to kill the whole family. Later, he got ready for church and from then on, he was fine.

He had calmed down, we watched television, and at about 11:15, he went to bed. Bernard came in at about 11:15 and put the television on to watch the late show. Dad, Dan, and I were sound asleep.

At about 12:30, Dad and Bernard heard him (Pat) scream. They both got up. Of course, Bernard got to him first and there he was in a very bad seizure. Bernard told Dad to call me because I knew what to do. By the time I was fully aware of everything, he was nearly out of bed and Bernard had all he could do to hold him down. I told Dan to give Bernard a spoon to hold Pat's tongue down and I ran to the phone and called the Rescue Squad. When they got here, Pat had passed out. They brought him around with the oxygen mask, but when he saw all the people around, he didn't know what happened and he was afraid of the mask, but he started shaking again, so they stuck the oxygen hose right in his mouth. We called the Doctor, and he ordered him to the Children's Hospital.

I went up there today and he doesn't look good at all. Tomorrow, they are going to have a brainwave taken and some X-rays. I will have more news for you tomorrow night and will write to you.

Wednesday.

I just called the hospital, and they were taking Patrick down for an EEG (brain wave/). The nurse said he was doing good, and his appetite was good. I thought he would never have another seizure, but I was wrong. I will let you know how he is as soon as I hear anything. Yesterday, he had X-rays of his head, neck, and chest. Today they did a blood sugar test this morning, and this afternoon, a brain wave.

The Doctor called and said that Pat can come home on Saturday. He is being put on phenobarbital (a sedative) three times a day. He hasn't had a conclusive reading on the brainwave but hopes to have it by the time he comes home on Saturday. He wants to keep tabs on Pat to try and find out what causes these seizures. The Doctor also said he was behaving up there in the hospital and that he is keeping himself busy waiting on other patients. This is all good news. Having a doctor determined to identify the cause of his seizures could be the answer. We are all encouraged. However, Pat's behavior once home adds more stress to Ma and Dad, who certainly do not need it anymore. Looking back, it is sad but engrossing that Pat is both the victim and the cause of tonic stress in our home.

Pat's persistence is rewarded! There was not a lot of good news in Pat's life, and so when it happened, Ma champions it for him.

July 20, 1962

Last Tuesday Pat went swimming at the pool. Every time he goes over there, he looks for his bike. Anyway, he never did get to swim because he saw his bike that was stolen. It had been painted gray and had been stripped down to nothing. He knew his frame number by heart. Somehow, he called the police. They came and told him that he would have to wait until the boy who had it came out of the pool, so he patiently waited (4 hours!). Finally, the boy came out. The policeman asked him about the bike, and he said he bought it from another boy about 2 or 3 weeks ago. So, the policeman took the bike to the #9 police station and told Pat to wait a couple of days until they checked it out. The next morning, a detective from Headquarters came out to the house and verified everything Pat told the police. He asked Pat if he had the bike. Pat said no, so he took Pat right down to the #9 police station and gave it to him. He *said the police should have given it to him yesterday. He knows the kid's name and address and we could press charges, but we do not have any witnesses, only Pat. We decided to leave well enough alone. I was so glad to have him get the bike back even though it doesn't look like the same bike we paid nearly $80 for.*

Ma's next two letters are very sad, leaving us all in great despair.

July 25, 1962

Dad has probably told you everything by now, but I want you to know that I know you and Jim did the right thing. This was coming for a long time. The morning he (Pat) attacked Dad, I called Dr. Colagno, and he suggested at that time admitting him to Meyer's Psychiatric Unit. I said no, what a fool I was. I have been hurting him and everyone around him for all these years. I'll never forgive myself. But I couldn't put him away when I would think how cute he was as a baby. All these years, I've put it off. Now, it is out of my hands, and I know we will all stick by him. I don't think he will ever come home again.

Pat losing control and physically attacking Dad was a shock, as was his subsequent admittance to the Psychiatric Unit at the medical center.

July 27, 1962

Dad and Jim were up to see Pat on Wednesday and he told me that Pat was OK but that he didn't know what day or time it was. I got so mad at Dad because I knew he hadn't told me everything. I've heard "through the grapevine" that Pat will be out in Gowanda today and that he has homicidal and suicidal tendencies. So, he needn't think he is fooling me. After the episode on Sunday, you know what we have been going through.

Pat lost control and tried to attack poor, debilitated Dad and then a few days later, he tried to attack Jim (our brother-in-law). No one was harmed and we took Pat to the E.J. Meyers Memorial Hospital, where they had a Psychiatric Unit as recommended by his Doctor. I think it was so ironic that the first of our family to visit Pat were the two people he attacked (Dad and Jim). This says a lot about their love and concern for him. After a few days in the Psychiatric Unit, a psychiatrist determined that Pat needed long-term treatment and he was then transported to the Gowanda State Hospital, the same facility where Dad spent three years of his life. I helped subdue Pat when he tried to attack Jim and was there for the transport of Pat to the hospital along with Jim, Bernie, and Tommy.

Based on Pat's behavior and my clinical experience today, I would guess he was diagnosed with Adolescent Adjustment Reaction with homicidal tendencies. What will all this do to Pat? He was only 15 years old. This was one of the worst days of all our lives. It also provides Pat with another ACE.

Chapter 15

The Mental Health Treatment System: Then and Now

Around the same time that Pat was admitted to the Gowanda State Hospital (1962), there was a coalescing of two other dissimilar events: Congress passed the Community Mental Health Services Act in 1963, and President Kennedy signed it into law. The intent of this law was to fund communities in the form of grants to help build Community Mental Health Centers where patients could receive psychiatric services while working and living at home rather than living in large institutions like the Gowanda State Hospital. Unfortunately, the law was underfunded, so the full intent of the law was never completely implemented.

The other event that surely convinced the public that the last thing they wanted for themselves and their loved ones was to be admitted to an institution, as portrayed in Ken Kesey's remarkable book *One Flew Over the Cuckoo's Nest (1992)*. This book and the 1975 movie of the same name starring Jack Nicholson clearly depicted the dismal state of mental health treatment of the 1940s, not the 1960s nor the vision of what the community mental health treatment system was hoping to become.

Pat and I had some common experiences with both the mental health systems of the 1950s when we visited our Dad when he was a patient at the same Gowanda State Hospital as Pat was in 1962. We saw the disorientation and confusion in Dad after he received a series of ECT (Electro-convulsive Therapy) treatments; the large "ward" in which he lived with 40 or 50 other men, and just the immensity and isolation of the institution itself with the capacity for over 3,000 patients.

Could Pat's admission to a psychiatric long-term care facility at such a young age (15) qualify as an ACE? Yes, of course it could. Just imagine as an adolescent being uprooted from your home and being admitted into a very large psychiatric institution 40 miles away from home. Ma's letter below provides some perspective on Pat's life during those difficult "adverse" days for him:

August 14, 1962

Last Sunday, Sue and Jim went out to the Gowanda State Hospital to see Pat. They said he was doing good. I won't be satisfied until I see him myself. Next Sunday, Bernard and Sharon (his girlfriend at the time) *are going out to see him in the afternoon. They are going to take a lunch. Now that Pat has outside privileges, they will take him down to the picnic grove and eat their lunch.*

As I said before I will have to see him myself. I am so glad that it is all over. I mean that he is being taken care of. Now, he really must take his pills. Tomorrow, he starts school. If he goes only 3 hours a day, he has a job to do. I don't know what it is because Peter couldn't remember. But if he goes all day, he won't have that job to do. One day or night last week, he was allowed to go to their dance. Another night, he was going to Bingo, and then he goes to Occupational Therapy every day, I think. I told Peter that Pat was making a whole new life for himself, and he told Sue & Jim he is having more fun out there than he ever had at home.

Ma, sadly, is resigned to the fact that there is nothing more she can do for Pat and that all her efforts in the past are now for naught. It was also very sad at home to scan his bedroom and see his stuff. He had very little. One of us will have to put it away, and it will probably be Ma. The rest of us lack the strength and fortitude to do it. It isn't that Pat died. He was seriously mentally ill, with what the psychiatrist said: "Pat has suicidal and homicidal tendencies and needs long-term care under supervision." That sounded like forever to me.

Back in the late 1960s, when I was undergoing my training to become an occupational therapist, I did a three-month internship in the same psychiatric unit at E.J. Meyer Memorial Hospital (now ECMC), where Pat was admitted prior to his transfer to the Gowanda State Hospital. In those days, about a third of occupational therapists worked in mental health (it is about 2% today), and I decided to join them. Upon graduation from the University at Buffalo's five-year OT program, I took my first position in the same Psychiatric Unit in ECMC (Erie County Medical Center), where my Dad, Pat, and some other family members were admitted for short stays. I also had an additional five years of clinical experience in an acute psychiatric care facility that included working with patients with substance abuse issues at Bry-Lin Hospitals in Buffalo, NY.

In the 1950s and 1960s, psychotropic medications expanded in use and effectiveness. Thus, patients with schizophrenia and other serious mental illnesses could be maintained without the use of physical restraints, and many could reside outside of an institution.

All patients always require supervision for the safety of all at the Gowanda State Hospital. There is a system in place there that allows more freedom and privileges for patients functioning at a higher level. This will be an adjustment for Pat, who is accustomed to coming and going where and when he chooses.

My family and I were all too familiar with the systems of supervision at Gowanda from when my Dad was a patient there, but that does not mean that we were looking forward to the depressing drive and anticipated challenging visits with Pat. As I read Ma's letters during Pat's days in Gowanda, I read them through the lens of an OT mixed in with the evolving and stagnating changes in the community mental health delivery system.

Note: Below is a letter from Tommy to Pat, but the date was not in it. The contents indicate that it was probably written in September of 1962, not long after Pat was admitted to Gowanda. He is coming home for a weekend, and they would not normally do this if his behavior was problematic or if he had only been there for a week or two.

Dear Pat,

Karoline and I are down in Rome, New York, and while she is busy trying to straighten out the shelves and books, I thought it would be a good time to drop you a line to enclose in your birthday card.

Everybody and everything is fine down here (Rome, NY). I guess you were surprised when you found out that you were coming home for the whole weekend. Jim was going to come out to pick you up on Friday, so be sure and thank him, won't you?

We will be hoping that you make this a happy weekend for Mom & Dad. You know they miss you and are lonely for you. Remember to take your pills on time and do what the Doctor advised you. Show everyone how you have improved so that you can return home for good soon.

I have got all our wood stashed away here in the cellar in a box, just awaiting your handiwork. We need another wall shelf. (Tommy drew a comical diagram of a slanted shelf).

Tommy was trying to coach Pat into not being a burden to Ma and Dad when he went home for the weekend. He also tried to bring in some humor to lighten Pat's days. Pat was allowed to come home

112

for the weekend and gave him the opportunity to celebrate his 16th birthday with the family.

Ma wrote the letters below, providing insights on how well Pat was doing: It was so strange to have Pat in the same psychiatric facility as Dad and us having the same stressful anticipations. How was Pat going to behave? Will he resist going back? Will he argue with Ma about what she writes on the form that had to be filled out upon his return? Dad always did this because what was written on the form about the patient's moods, interaction, cooperation, appearance, and overall behavior was reviewed by the staff. What was written on the form was one of the factors used to determine a patient's privileges, independence, future visits home, and eventual discharge.

Not surprisingly, Pat followed Dad's routine: he was miserable and withdrawn during the visit and then aggressively pressured Ma not to put anything negative on the form. As with Dad, Pat's weekend visits were always viewed with some trepidation by us all. Ma's letter below lets Tommy know how Pat was doing.

September 12, 1962

How did Pat sound on the phone? He was good while he was home but very resentful and depressed. He knew I had that paper to fill out while he was home. He asked me 3 times what I was going to put on the paper. The same as Dad used to ask.

He didn't give us any trouble. Peter took him with him a couple of times. Bernard drove him over to Greg's house and he brought Greg back for supper. I thought he would enjoy him. He didn't say whether he enjoyed the visit or not. He also went over to Sue and Jim's today. I guess they were going for a ride this afternoon. Bernard said he would take him back tonight. Pat says he doesn't want to go back to that G_ _ D_ _ place, but he knows he must.

During this time, I could never get past the fact that at 15 years of age, Pat was a patient in the Gowanda State Hospital. What sort of ACE would this experience forge at his young age? How ill was he? Difficult? Yes, but the label of "mentally ill with homicidal and suicidal tendencies" did not seem to fit. I could still not go into his bedroom and see his stuff without crying. I cannot imagine what this whole thing was doing to Ma and Dad. For my Dad, it must have been emotional torture to realize that his youngest son was now walking the same path he walked for three years. As can be seen in the excerpt below, Ma has her own torture:

October 14, 1962

I just got back from Gowanda. Peter and I went out. I got quite a shock. My friend (Pat) is back up on the sixth floor. (The higher floor that a patient was placed in dictated their privileges and level of independence allowed). *He ran away Tuesday; he and some other kid. Pat said when the Doctor told him to go back up on the sixth floor, he (Pat) said he might as well hang himself. So now he must wear their clothes and no belt. Last Sunday, when he was home, he threatened to run away and I told him that wasn't going to help him any, but he said he didn't care; he hated the place. As soon as he saw me, he started to cry, and of course, I did too. I felt so bad for him. First, he said he had to stay up there for 6 months, but later he said he was only up there for 1 week or 2, and then he didn't know how long he would be up there.*

This week, before he came home, he had an argument with some other boy in school. When they got outside, the two of them started fist-fighting, and Pat went into a seizure. He lay on the ground for about 10 minutes, and then they carried him inside. He didn't want them to tell the Doctor, so whether he knew about the fight and seizure or not, I don't know.

Today, while we were sitting in the room visiting, some young boy came and asked me for a cigarette. I gave it to him. After he left, Pat said he had had a fight with him last night. We knew that the more of these incidents that Pat was involved in, the longer it was going to be before he would be home for good. It seemed to us that he was incapable of controlling his temper and frustrations.

Here's Ma:

October 31, 1962
I have been thinking about Pat all week. Sue and Jim are going out there on Sunday. I would like to go along because I have a feeling he has had the shock treatment. I would like to see just how he is responding to them. Dad says he had about 3 a week. Sunday, when we were out there, while Bernard and Peter went to the store for us, you should have heard how he (Pat) talked. He was blaming everyone for him being there and he also said we would all get paid back for putting him in there. I didn't tell Bernard or Peter what he said because I knew they would get mad at him.

Finally, some positive news about Pat:

December 12, 1962
PS Dad and Peter went out to see Pat on Sunday. He is fine. He mops the floors and makes beds over in another wing and when the linen comes up on his floor, he puts it all away. Dad said he was good and looked good, too.

Is Pat getting close to being discharged? See below:

February 4, 1963
Yesterday, Sue and Jim drove out to Gowanda to see Pat. He had called Saturday to say he might be coming home for good, but I had to talk to Dr. Gorlicki. When Sue and Jim left, I told them to tell Pat

I would call the Doctor today. He (Pat) wanted Sue to see the Doctor yesterday, but there were so many people waiting to see him she said to let me talk to the Doctor today. I was waiting for my washer to stop, so I decided to call out there instead of waiting until today. The Doctor said he (Pat) had been very good and had quieted down considerably and next Friday (the 8th), Jim is going to go out there, pick him up and he can be home for 10 days. If he behaves while he is home at that time, they are going to release him. Of course, he will be under Convalescent Care and will have to report every so often.

Pat is showing some maturity and motivation to do better with his life, and Ma wisely does not say what is on her mind:

Dad died unexpectedly on April 24, 1963, at just 54 years of age. It may seem strange to say unexpectedly when he was so debilitated and still smoked three packs a day, but it was still a shock to us all. I found it so sad to carry a small shopping bag of Dad's clothes, slippers, and wallet home the day he died and to see his empty chair and reading light turned off. We are all a mess, and anyone in the family 18 years or younger (Danny and Pat) could readily add another ACE over the loss of Dad.

Maybe not so good news about Pat:

February 13, 1963
Bernard and I started for Gowanda this morning, but the snowstorm was getting worse the further south we drove. We didn't even get to Hamburg, and we had been on the road 1 hour then, so we turned around and came back. At about 2, Pat called and was beginning to worry for fear we had forgotten about him. I explained to him, and he said OK, he understood. He called Thursday to say he could come home, but I had to talk to his Doctor Gorlicki first. So, I called him, and he said no, not for a while. He also said Pat shouldn't go

anywhere by himself when he is home. I asked who was going to tell
him and he said he would. Ma did not want to be the bearer of bad
news. Who could blame her?

October 24, 1963
Big news for Pat and the rest of us as well. After 16 months of
hospitalization in the Gowanda State Hospital, on October 24, 1963,
Pat was finally discharged. It was so good to have him home. He
was very happy and a big help to Ma. He wants to get a job, but
without a high school diploma, it will not be easy.

Also, in the Fall of 1963, Tommy and Ma agreed to take advantage
of an opportunity that Dad's insurance provided. They decided to
use the insurance money to buy a house for Ma and Pat and
everyone else in the family who needed a place to live. The house
payments, taxes, and any major repairs would be paid for by
Tommy, and this would greatly reduce the economic stress that both
Ma and Pat were experiencing. The house that Ma and Tommy
decided on was a new-built, three-bedroom ranch in a very pleasant,
new, suburban neighborhood. Pat also proved to be very handy and
resourceful in repairing things he was unfamiliar with by consulting
some neighbors. This whole arrangement with the new house would
prove far more beneficial to the family than we could have ever
imagined (see Ma's subscription below):

Because of the marital troubles Sue and Jim were having, they split
up. Thank goodness we had the room here for Sue, Kathleen, and
Shawn to move in here at 79 Marilyn Drive. Kathleen transferred
to St John Vianney school, and Sue is looking for a job. The boys
get a big kick out of Shawn.

One little bright spot for Pat, but with a sad aspect as described by Ma:

February 15, 1964

Pat worked last week one day for Jim and made $10. He owed seven of it because he wanted to go see the "New Christy Minstrels" Thursday night. I gave him $3 to go up there to Kleinihan's Music Hall to see them and Sue had loaned him $1 a way back. We both loved this group, and I regret not going with him. But he again went alone but still enjoyed the concert very much.

March 6, 1964

Pat had another job in the nearby Plaza, but he only worked 2 days. They let him go because another boy came in and had experience in the shoe business. I think they thought he would work into selling shoes, but not in two days. I presumed they knew, and after that, he was dusting off boxes. He didn't bother going back at all until tomorrow, when he gets paid. Just don't mention anything in your letter about this. He is getting very discouraged.

Pat valiantly tried to find a job and he was willing to take any job. He worked as a dishwasher stockboy, selling magazine descriptions door-to-door and helping in my brother-in-law Jim's gas station. Unfortunately, all of these were temporary jobs, and he was laid off after only a few weeks. I did his taxes that year and he showed real perseverance because he had 13 W-2 forms for each of his former employers. He wanted and needed a full-time regular job for financial and self-esteem reasons, but nothing stuck. Ma saw what this was doing to him but didn't know how to help him.

March 20, 1964

Pat went uptown today for a job he saw advertised in the paper last night. Tomorrow, he starts selling Life magazine door-to-door along with 2 other books.

I remember well when he came home exhausted from walking continuously almost all-day ringing doorbells without any sales. It was a job that only paid commissions on sales, and of course, no sales equals no pay. He did find humor in the corny message they trained him to say, and he had us all laughing uproariously as he ran through his pitch. One day without pay was enough for him. He called the guy that hired him and quit the next day.

To say that Pat's environment was in flux would be an understatement. For all of us, our lives got a little more complicated when Sue, Kathleen, and Shawn joined Ma, Pat, Bernie, and me in a small house with one bathroom. Sound familiar? It was similar in size to the home that Sue and Jim owned and welcomed us in twice. This time, it was far more fun than it was stressful because I always looked forward to having all the people I loved under one roof. I doubt Pat felt the same.

April 4, 1964

Sue and Jim found an upper flat on Roanoke Parkway in South Buffalo and got back together. They will be moving on the 15th of April. They also bought a 1962 Corvair. (The Corvair's alleged problems stemmed from its unusual rear-engine layout and the suspension that held it up. That design led to unstable emergency handling, according to Ralph Nader. It's hard to say whether the Corvair was much more dangerous than other cars of its time, but this car was problematic for Jim and Sue for as long as they owned it. But Jim was in denial about it, and this gave Pat plenty of ammunition for his humorous comments to us, not to Jim).

Sue gave me her car (not the Corvair). As much as I use it, I figured it was worth it. Now, I can go to church when I want to and go to the cemetery. We are having a high mass for Dad on the 24th of April, and I am having memoriam put into the newspaper for the 24th. I will send one to you. There has been so much that has happened to all of us since Dad passed away. I hope he is watching over us and helping us get back to regular living again.

I will be lonesome when Sue goes, but I know it is best for her and for all of us. There will be a lot of cleaning up to do in the cellar and the changing of furniture. I am going to try and buy paint for the cellar. I think if we can get some cement for that one hole and then paint it, the paint will act as a sealer. I want to get some bushes and rose bushes to plant.

We missed them all when they moved out, but just like Ma, we knew it was for the best. It is a calm house with just Ma, Bernie, Pat, and me at home. Ma is worried about Pat and his inability to get and keep jobs. There was also the dilemma that if Pat does become employed, then that would reduce Dad's pension for Ma significantly. It is amazing how Ma and Pat's lives are so intertwined.

April 18, 1964
Pat is so disgusted with himself and his life. I really feel sorry for him, but since December, he has had 5 jobs. One of the men on one of his jobs told me he can't take responsibility. I have contacted the Railroad Retirement Board and explained to them the situation. They are going to contact Gowanda, and I must take him up there some day next week. I don't say he can't work, but I do say he couldn't hold a steady job. I don't know how I am going to explain it to him when they question him or want him to go before some head-shrinker. I couldn't spell it.

I forgot to tell you Pat has another job! He went over to the dock where Jimmy used to work and got hired. They told him to be home on Sunday and they would call and tell him when to come to work, I mean what time. I worked one night at this same dock, and I found it too grueling. I quit after 6 hours or so. I don't know if Pat will be able to take it. Each time Pat was rejected by a potential employer or lost a job, it just continued the pummeling process.

Big news! Sometime in early 1966, Pat found a full-time job at a paint factory where Danny also worked. The work is steady, and he is learning a lot about making paint. He has a good salary, benefits like health insurance, paid days off, and he gets periodic raises. It is amazing the transformation in him. He is so happy, confident, and very careful with his money. He is helping Ma a lot and bought her a new living room set and himself a color TV that he will have all paid off in six months.

A problem did arise when he had a seizure at work while working on one of the large mixing machines. The company wanted to lay him off because of safety concerns, but Pat got the union to fight for him. Here is what Ma said about this and some other issues at Pat's job:

May 29, 1966
Pat went to see Dr. Zoll (his neurologist) with one of the men from the Union. Dr. Zoll wrote a letter to the company stating that Pat could run the machine. So now he should be a general Operator with an increase in pay.

July 4, 1966, A good day!
Yesterday, Pat went to a picnic at Chestnut Ridge. His plant had it. He was playing ball and won a prize for being the most popular guy there. He also won hot dogs, rolls, and hamburgers. Every time I

heard of Pat being happy and staying employed, it made me extremely happy, but not as happy as Ma. She saw how being unemployed diminished him greatly.

July 7, 1966, A not so good day!
We are all fine here, except Pat. On the 4th of July evening, the family came out for a cookout. The boys were playing football in the backyard. Pat twisted his ankle and fell. I couldn't feel any broken bones, but it was starting to swell. I wanted one of the boys to take him over to the hospital, but he said no, that he'll be alright. They left about 10 and his ankle was 3 times the ordinary size. The neighbors were sitting outside, so I called them in to look at it. One of them was a nurse and Bob Luthringer was with them, so he took Pat to the hospital. They taped it up for him and X-rayed the foot. He has a bad sprain, but he had a fit because he just got a raise and a promotion. He is now a General Foreman.

August 15, 1966, Ma's pride in Pat being employed is wonderful to see and hear!
Pat is working from 4:30 P.M. to 1 A.M. now and has gotten another raise. He sure is doing good over there, and he really enjoys the work. When he was on days, he was teaching the new men how to mix the paint and how to run the machines. I am very proud of him.

September 15, 1966
Last night Pat and I went to Bernard's and Anne Marie's for supper and the evening. Bernard went over to the K of C for the evening. Bernard joined last night. After February, he and Peter are going to take the 3rd degree. Pat wants to join too, but not being able to get out to St John Vianney church, he will have a hard time getting a letter. But I suppose there is a way of getting around that, too. I

122

remember Pat joining the K of C, but I don't remember recruiting him. Bernie must have convinced him to join. Either way, I'm glad he did.

December 8, 1966, More stress for Ma and Pat from an unexpected source. *Pat went back to work yesterday. With the money he got for his vacation, he bought a new suit and coat with a zip-in lining and, some new underwear and a new shirt. He looks nice when he dresses up.*

Last night, Pat was in bed, and I was just going to get ready for bed when someone pounded on the back door (11 P.M.). I went and who was it but my brother. He was so drunk that he couldn't even talk. I told him I was going to bed. I cleaned off the front bed for him. Well, he went, but he laid down with all his clothes on, including his shoes and rubbers. He talked, laughed, and pounded on the walls until I got so nervous I couldn't stand it. So, I called Bernard to come and get him and take him home. He did. I felt bad, but when he comes here drunk, that is all. I can't stand it.

Pat paid for his television in 7 months ($500). This Saturday, he is going to have his antennae put up. I will let you know how his colored TV works on Sunday.

August 13, 1967
Pat lost his job at the paint factory and is very depressed. I do not know what caused Pat to lose his job, but it sure was devastating for him, Ma, and the rest of us who want so much for him to be successful.

August 28, 1967
Pat got a job down at the place where Danny works, the Wilson Warehouse. He was so excited about it that he was still roaming

around the house at 2 A.M. I hope everything works out for him now. I think he realizes now that jobs are not so plentiful.

January 31, 1967, Great fun for all!
Last night we (Jim, Sue, Janice, Pat, and I) went to Bingo. Of course, we didn't win. But last week Pat said he wasn't coming anymore, so Sunday night I said that I wouldn't be home tomorrow night (last night, Monday) because I was going to Susan's for supper and then to Bingo. He said he was through; he couldn't stand it anymore. I got through work and took the bus to Susan's. At about 5:00 P.M., the back door opened, and Sue said I wondered if that was Pat. I told her no, that he wouldn't be coming. The back door opened and who was it, but Pat. He said he was on the Orchard Park bus and when it came to Stevenson Street, the bus stopped, and the bus driver said this is as far as you go so he got off. We had a lot of laughs. I said if he ever went to Bingo and won, he probably would have a seizure and couldn't holler. I am going to quit now. I must take a bath and get ready for work.

Reference

Kesey, Ken. *One Flew Over the Cuckoo's Nest.* Penguin Putnam (1992).

Chapter 16

Ma's "Refuge"

When Tommy and Ma came up with the idea to acquire a home where our family would always have a place where they could live without the ominous presence of landlords or landladies, they never could have imagined how well it would all work out. The decision to purchase a new house in a suburban area not too far from our sister Sue's home and Pat's work also worked out well. So, 79 Marilyn Drive, West Seneca, NY, became our family's "Refuge." We never called it that, but Tommy always did right from the beginning.

Why "The Refuge?" While Tommy never offered a definition of "refuge," the words associated with our new house were so appropriate: shelter, sanctuary, retreat, safety, security, harbor, haven, and stronghold. The primary occupants of the home were Ma and Pat, and they proved to be great stewards of "The Refuge." These two were also the primary caretakers, and they were very good at it. We all pitched in on big projects like painting the inside and outside of the house, planting the lawn, and so forth, but the day-to-day maintenance was all the responsibility of Ma and Pat.

When we first moved in, Dad had, of course, died, and Danny was in the Navy. So, that left Ma, Pat, Bernie, and me, who lived in "The Refuge" until Bernie and I married. However, it was seldom just us. Whenever members of our extended family needed a home, Ma always welcomed them into "The Refuge" without calling it that. I counted 15 of my family members who called "The Refuge" home at different times over the seven years Ma lived there, and some moved in and out two or three times. It was a bit chaotic at times, but in general, it was fun because, many times, we had new babies or little kids to play with, and the peace it brought to troubled family members made it all worthwhile.

I think the reason it worked out with families coming and going was Ma's welcoming presence. She always said that she "loved a house full," and she meant it. Anyone who came to Ma's "Refuge" just naturally assumed that they would help with cooking, shopping, snow shoveling, cleaning, washing dishes, and whatever else Ma needed to do.

Were there any downsides to "The Refuge." Yes, there were a few big ones. The distance from "The Refuge" and my sister Sue's home in South Buffalo was a problem. Ma did not have a car, and this posed a problem for getting to her job at the local Sears store and to get in to visit with Sue. With Sue working full-time, she did not have a lot of free time to make the drive to Ma's as much as they both would have liked. Ma and Sue were the individual and collective glue that kept our family together through the most difficult of times. They needed frequent face-to-face contact for mutual support, and time and distance were now problems.

Another problem with time and distance was Pat's job. He has worked steadily for a few years at a warehouse that was about 4 miles away. His schedule was often out of sync with the local bus schedule, and he could not drive because of his epilepsy. Also, it was infrequent that he could ride with a co-worker because few of them lived near "The Refuge." He often had to resort to hitchhiking and walking to and from work. It was wonderful seeing Pat having a steady job, and we all worried that not having transportation may prevent him from keeping it.

Ma was in the same situation as Pat in terms of needing transportation to and from her job at Sears and for shopping. She worked 40 hours a week with erratic hours that, like Pat, were out of sync with the bus schedule. Luckily, she was not shy about asking for rides, but there were several days when a taxi was her only alternative.

Ma's "loving a houseful" sometimes worked against her because she never said "no" to anyone in the family who wanted to come for dinner or needed a place to live. Her health was declining, but she refused to let it limit contact with her family, and this was a somewhat hidden detriment. We really did not know how very impaired she was becoming because she seldom complained.

There were periodic stressful times when something needed to be repaired, and it was on Ma and Pat to get it done. Both Ma and Pat proved very resourceful at finding temporary fixes and utilizing helpful neighbors when necessary. Pat quickly demonstrated his mechanical problem-solving skills and frequently saved Tommy the cost of an expert plumber, painter, electrician, carpenter, and so forth.

Despite these sometimes seemingly insurmountable problems, "The Refuge" worked. It worked for just over seven years mainly because of Ma and Pat's diligence as caretakers and their flexibility with the comings and goings of family members.

Chapter 17

Pat's Best Years

The best that I saw Pat function was during the time he worked at the Wilson Warehouse, initially as a laborer and later as a Towmotor or Forklift Driver, which he loved. He earned a good salary and benefits. This latter job further transformed Pat. It not only greatly improved his standard of living and quality of life, but it markedly enhanced his self-esteem and self-concept. He worked hard and getting to and from the job was not easy. However, these did not deter the good feelings he derived from his proudly telling people, "I'm a Towmotor Driver at the Wilson Warehouse." He stood straighter and spoke with greater confidence each time he said it. We were all very proud of him.

With his earnings, he was able to take our nephew Shawn to California on vacation, where they went to Disneyland and visited Tommy and Karoline. He also went by himself on a bus trip to the Great Smoky Mountains and another bus trip (also alone) to New York City, where he toured all the usual sites.

He also helped "The Refuge" by buying Ma a portable dishwasher, which she loved, and for the house, a lawn mower and snow blower that he used to keep the lawn cut and driveway clear. However, he also treated himself to things he always wanted but could never afford, like a color TV, a stereo, and a guitar that he learned to play with lessons. He also enhanced his wardrobe with new clothes whenever he wanted.

Pat loved showing me the latest things he bought, repaired, adapted, salvaged, or was given by a neighbor. He saved Tommy quite a bit of money over the seven years Tommy had "The Refuge."

These were indeed the most productive and happiest years of Pat's life. His ACEs had far less sway in Pat's life in his era of relative prosperity.

His seizures also seemed more controlled due to some radical neurosurgery he had done and to the diligent taking of his medications that were closely titrated by the ever-conscientious Doctor Zoll. There were still periodic "sick spells" and occasional mild seizures, but thankfully, these did not impede his work or other activities. His life was good!

The following letters of Ma's attest to how well Pate was functioning during his most productive years and how proud she was of him. Here are Pat and Ma being their usual productive selves and enjoying life. There is no mention of seizures, calls for the Rescue Squad or leg pain!

October 22, 1967
Pat is painting the ceiling in my room today. It will take quite a while to get this painting business done because he can only do it on the weekends. He works quite hard during the week, so I can't expect him to do much then. I would love to help him, but painting must affect me in some way or the other. The last time I painted, I ended up in the hospital for 6 weeks. Maybe it is the up and down with the arm that does it. I don't know.

Today is a beautiful day. Sun shining but cold. I have the furnace at 65 degrees because I will be getting supper shortly and that heats up the house quite a bit.

Today being Sunday, I didn't do much at all. Got up at 7:40, had my breakfast, read the paper, started my 6 loads of wash, cleaned out two cupboards in the kitchen, washed all the woodwork in my bedroom, took all the clothes out of the closet, and washed that inside and out. Now, I am going to start my chicken. I am having fried chicken, mashed potatoes, cauliflower, asparagus, chicken gravy, coffee, and cookies. How does that sound? I'm sitting here, writing, smoking, and on my second bottle of beer. It is tragic that Ma is still smoking!

Ma is showing her wit in the second paragraph and her delight in having this family group for dinner that she prepared:

October 31, 1967
Yesterday, Peter, Janice, Aunt Florence, Bernard, Anne Marie, and Jill came for dinner. I made lasagna. It was very good, and they all enjoyed it very much. We ate early because Bernard doesn't like to drive the Thruway at night with Anne Marie and the baby, so they left about 5 or maybe a little earlier. Peter, Janice, and Aunt Florence stayed till about 7:30. Peter had to go to work last night, otherwise, they would have stayed a while longer.

On Thursday, Susan will be 38 years old. We don't buy each other anything, the whole family, I mean, but her being my best-looking daughter, I broke down and bought her a pretty tea pot. She had mentioned it some time ago, so I kept it in the back of my head until today.

Ma's health continues to improve, and Pat is gathering data and ideas from a friendly neighbor. Both Pat and Ma enjoy taking care of and improving "The Refuge." They have no overnight family members at present, so they can relax a bit.

November 1, 1967
I went to the Doctor today. He took my pressure and said it was fine, listened to my heart, and said it was a slow, even beat. He said I have come a long way in seven years since those two attacks I had in 1960. I got my flu shot and he said that they (the medical people) are expecting a flu epidemic this winter. So, he gave me my booster

shot. Now my arm is sore. But I don't care if I don't get sick like I was in July. That was terrible. I didn't think I was going to live out that week.

Pat was talking to the man down the street and was asking him about paneling. The man said they have a new kind that can be glued on, and if Pat decides to do it himself, he will lend Pat all the tools he needs, even the electric saw. I said no thanks. That's all need to hear is the saw going and Pat hollering, "Look, Ma, no fingers." Pat said he wouldn't tackle it, but we will have it done by someone. I am also thinking of papering the one side where my telephone is and buying a new electric refrigerator. Right now, the new refrigerator is a dream, but who knows what can materialize.

"The Refuge" has some "guests," Ma gets a bit crazy and visits a spiritualist who has disturbing news for "someone." Also, Pat buys a snowblower for "The Refuge" and plows the next-door neighbor's driveway in return for past favors. Ma has her usual busy day without pain or complaints:

Chapter 18

Ma's Health: Part I

"It was the best of times; it was the worst of times...." For some reason, *in* writing this section, I have the beginning of this phrase from Charles Dickens's *A Tale of Two Cities* running through my mind. Of course, the whole passage doesn't fit Ma's life in those days, but those first few words certainly do. For Ma, *The best of times* occurred with every family gathering or even just a visit by any one of us. It was also *the best of times* whenever life's circumstances caused family members to stay at Ma's "Refuge." She loved it, especially her grandbabies. *The worst times* were when her pain was so terrible that her normal activities had to be curtailed or even stopped. A good example she gave me was that during her two-block walk to the bus stop, she had to time it just right. If the pain was too great, she would be unable to step up to board the bus and then must step back and wave the driver on. Waiting for the next bus usually made her late for work. If it was a bitterly cold and wintry day, going to the bus stop earlier was a problem because of her shortness of breath. This pattern of exertion-excruciating pain-ceasing activity was the way she had to live her life. Being a "get'er done" kind of person, this type of thing drove her crazy.

Another aspect of *the worst of times* for Ma was the economic necessity for her to have to work full-time. Being in her late 50s and with two very limiting medical conditions dealing with her heart and her poor circulation, her job is proving to be too much for her. I called her almost every night at 11:00 o'clock and she usually tells me how being on her feet throughout her shift is so painfully difficult. At home, it is not much of a problem because she can sit down anytime she needs to, but this is not the case at work.

Salespeople are expected to always be on their feet, ready to serve the customers. The pension she receives from Dad's railroad pension is just not adequate to cover all her living expenses. So, work full time, she must.

Her doctor referred Ma to a vascular surgeon who specializes in treating conditions like Ma's. I went with her to hear about a surgery he does that could help Ma a great deal. Because the large femoral arteries in her upper legs are so obstructed, they need to be surgically removed and replaced with tubes made of some synthetic material. It sounded good, so Ma agreed to have it done. In a week or two, they will schedule her for this radical surgery. Hopefully, it will be as effective to the extent the surgeon says. Getting rid of her pain would be wonderful.

The surgery did take place on March 18, and the letter below, written by Tommy to Karoline back in California, explains what took place:

March 18, 1968
They moved Ma from the Intensive Care ward to a semi-private, semi-recovery-type room. The Doctors said she is not out of the woods yet and that she is still in a semi-critical condition. Before she was moved, they let me in to see her. It was hard to control myself. You know me. But I had to because she does not realize how close she came to the end. They told us she stopped breathing on the operating table, and they had to give her mouth-to-mouth resuscitation to keep her going. Then, that heart attack almost finished her off. I was, of course, shocked when I first saw her. She looked so gray and small in that big bed. Peter had prepared her somewhat for me to come in, but she still went all to pieces when she saw me. I calmed her down and we had a nice chat. Then, they moved her downstairs to another room. Wasson, Bernard, and I visited with her and Jimmy for the rest of the afternoon until Sue

134

arrived; then we went home. But you know it is like you said- Ma is a strong woman. A week ago, today, she was operated on and nearly died. I was amazed at her alertness yesterday and her eagerness to get well. It was a miracle what they did for her. Right now, we are sweating out a relapse. If she makes it to Sunday, I'll start making plans to return right away.

What I would like to do is to leave here next Wednesday (27 March) and try to be home by the following Friday or Saturday, depending upon when I can get out of McGuire, which will be on a space-available basis. I would like to be home by next weekend. But I don't want to leave here too early for fear I might have to turn right around and come back because she had a relapse or suffered an attack or pneumonia. I feel useless here, but the family, especially Sue, who has been under terrific strain with Jim and Ma laid up, are glad that I am here. I think after a week that I can have Ma brain-washed about the necessity for me to go home as soon as possible. It will be better all-around, though, if I am satisfied that she is on the road to recovery before I leave. Another thing, too, is that I am out here with Pat so that he is not alone during this period when he is upset. This makes Ma feel better that there is someone here in case he has a seizure or some other trouble.

I also want to be able to make sure that there is a reasonable plan as to where Ma is going to stay after she comes out of the hospital. Tentatively, it looks like she will come here with Pat, and Anne Marie will come down from Rochester and stay here and take care of her. That would be the ideal solution and I am pushing it.

About Ma's operation, it looks like the tubes in her legs (femoral arteries) *are working alright, the doctor said, because her feet are warm and have a healthy color. Ma said before the operation, her feet were always cold and now they are warm as toast. Keep your fingers crossed.*

Ma did well after the surgery and convalesced at our house for two or three days before going home to "The Refuge." Anne Marie came in from Rochester and stayed with Ma for another three days, and by then, Ma was fine. In no time at all, Ma was back to her old self, welcoming all visitors, especially those of us who showed up with her grandkids. I think we were all thinking the same thing.: We almost lost Ma, so let's take advantage of every opportunity to spend time with her. We came together almost every Sunday to watch football on Pat's color TV, and sometimes also during the week to take Ma to the doctor's or to do her shopping. We all kept the good times rolling with our jokes and comments. I really miss those days.

Ma went to see her primary care doctor and he had some sobering news for her about the necessity of her surgery. Ma and Pat's health and employment statuses are intertwined in a synergistic way. All is good when they both are working. So, in Ma's view, she must return to work as soon as possible, and getting clearance for this visit is key. See the doctor's clear and ominous message below:

June 4, 1968
I didn't want to finish this letter until I went to see Dr. Yerkovich. Today, I went and he told me that if they had waited two more months, I would have lost both of my legs because gangrene had already set in. That's why I haven't been able to walk outside. I can walk in the house and up and down stairs, but today, he said I should try my legs. So tomorrow, if the weather stays nice (it's supposed to go to 80 degrees), I will go out and try walking. When I think about what could have happened, I really get scared. He also said no more work until September. That is OK because my disability goes on until October. That is the month I go and apply for my Railroad Retirement.

Ma is progressing nicely, as she indicates below, with her "new legs working just fine!"

August 20, 1968
Saturday afternoon, Sue, Jim, Shawn, Patrick, and I all went to the Hamburg Fair. We left here about 5 P.M. and got home around 10:30 or 11. Pat and Shawn went on a few rides, Jim and Pat tried their hands at trying to win something, but the only thing they won was Pat putting a ring around a quart of Pepsi and Jimmy won a plaque for Shawn's bedroom wall because the fellow was about 20# off on guessing Jimmy's weight. We went through all of the buildings, and I walked all over. My legs held up beautifully, with no aches and no pain.

When Ma went to see her regular doctor again for a follow-up, he had some interesting but annoying information for her. See the excerpt below:

August 28, 1968
Yesterday, I went to Dr. Yerkovich, and he gave me a clean bill of health. He also told me I was being written up in one of the medical journals here, and next month (September), I will be under discussion at Mercy Hospital. He didn't say if he wanted me there or not, but Peter said sometimes, when a patient is under discussion like that with other doctors, the patient is asked to be present. He didn't say anything about that, so I guess I won't have to be there. He always asked me if I was walking. When I told him that I went to the Fair and walked all around and could have gone around again, he said, "Isn't that fantastic when you think of how bad you were last year." Then he had the nerve to say, "Aren't you glad that I told you to go to the hospital?" I said yes, but all the time, I felt like telling him why something wasn't done before when I was

complaining for 2 years. But of course, I didn't say anything, because he has been good to me. I guess I can excuse one mistake.

The two letters below show how engaged Ma was in family activities. They also show her high level of mental acuity, mobility without pain, and endurance, which is surprising considering her history of cardiac and vascular impairments. She always felt responsible for keeping Tommy and Karoline informed about the family, and no detail was too small to leave out:

October 14, 1967
I received your letter and was glad to hear that everyone is OK. We are all fine here.

You were a little ahead of yourself when you said that Bernard was all moved. They packed last night, and they leave today. Bernard came home Friday night (last night). Peter, Danny, Pat, and he loaded the truck. Bernard had to be back in Rochester this morning by 9:30 for a meeting. So, Jim, Shawn and Pat will drive the truck down. Peter had to work last night, so he left his car at Susan's this morning and took Jim's car. Sue is driving his car down with Danny, Anne Marie, and Jill. By the way, their new address will be <u>91 Loden Lane, Rochester, N.Y.</u> I don't have the Zip Code number, but as soon as I get it, I will pass it on to you. I know it sounds a little complicated, but I am writing fast because I must leave in about 5 minutes to catch my bus. I will continue it later.

October 19, 1967
Yesterday was my day off, so I went into Susan's and helped her move downstairs. We moved all the dishes, pots, and pans and did all the cupboards. First, though, I stopped off to see David and Lisa. They are real cute babies. They both ran and wanted to be picked up, loved, and kissed. Then I went to Susan's. Pat came for supper and after that, he and Jim (after Jim came from work) moved the

living room furniture down. Kathleen brought all the drapes, and she and I hung them. I don't know if I told you before, but Sue and Jim bought Bernard's living room rug, runner, stove, and refrigerator. A man is coming Monday to buy her old stove, refrigerator, and the refrigerator she got from Peter for nothing. He said he would take all three off her hands for $100. Not bad, I don't think for a stove and refrigerator that are 17 years old.

Ma has a beau now named Steve. He was married to my Godmother, who died several years ago. She mentions him in her next letter.

November 26, 1967
Friday, I went over to the plaza at 9, went to the Your Host restaurant to have my breakfast, caught the 9:20 bus to the foot Doctor, got back to the plaza at 11, went into Sears, had my lunch and was on the floor at 12 and worked until 9. I then caught the other 9:20 P.M. bus over to the grocery store and did my shopping for the week, called a cab, and was home at 10:15. What a day! Saturday, I worked 9-6, came home, ate my dinner, and read the paper. Steve called and wanted to know if I would like to go out and go through the new stores out here, one on Southwestern Blvd. and one on Union Road. I said yes so when we got there, he told me to pick out my Christmas present, so I did: 3 blouses and 2 skirts. It was only about 9 or so, so we went in to visit Danny for about one and a half hours. Then we went and had a few beers ourselves and I was in bed at 11:45. Today, Pat and I went into Susan's for another turkey dinner. Pat brought the two legs home with him. This Sunday, Sue, Jim, Shawn, Wasson, Peter, and Janice are coming for dinner. Pat's appetite is fine.

Anne Marie was not only married to my brother Bernie, but she was also my wife Janice's sister. So, things like the following were of major concern to us all:

The week before last, Anne Marie, Bernard and the baby stayed here. Sunday morning, when we all got up, Anne Marie was crying. You know 5 years ago, she had an operation on her ear that was her 3rd operation. It is a tumor that keeps coming back. So that Sunday, she discovered that she had another lump. The next day, she went to the Doctor, and she must have another operation. Another tumor has come back, so she will be operated on January 16th. I am really worried about her, and of course, we are all concerned. They always do a biopsy of it.

Well, Peter has been at the Buffalo General Hospital all week and last week, and in between, he has been at Meyers Hospital. This coming week, he is going to the Children's Hospital and next Saturday, he must spend the day at Perrysburg. That used to be a T.B. Hospital, but now it is a state hospital.

I have been feeling good; only my legs are beginning to give me trouble. I guess it's arthritis. When I walk down from the house to get the bus, I can hardly get my foot up on the curb, so I go down and up driveways. If the bus ever came along as soon as I got there, I would never make it up on the step. So that is why I leave a little bit early so I can walk slowly and then have time to rest a little bit early, so I can walk slowly and then have time to rest my legs. Sometimes, it feels like my legs have come out of their sockets. I told the Doctor about it and he had me x-rayed, but the only thing that he could find out was arthritis.

Ma had a stressful beginning to her day on December 5th, but a very positive day with a bit of a warning two days later it was December 7th ("Pearl Harbor Day"):

Yesterday I had an awful scare. I always check my purse in the morning to make sure I have money, a door key, etc., and I couldn't find my card case that holds all identification, charge plates, hospitalization cards, pictures, etc. I looked until I was blue in the

140

face. I finally had to stop looking and go to work. I inquired over there, but no good. I decided to wait until I got home and then go through everything again. At about 5, Pat called and asked if I was missing a card case. I nearly fell over. It seems Saturday night when Bernard picked me up, he took me to this new place on Abbott Road, namely "Jacobi's." I must have taken it out of my purse to show him something and somehow dropped it or left it on the table. Pat said the man there wanted me to call him, so I did. He had to have verification, and he was asking me questions, so tonight, when I get through with work, I am going to ask this girl who is going to drive me home if she will take me over there so I can get it.

A raise and an admonishment for Ma!

December 7, 1967
Today is the anniversary of Pearl Harbor. How well I remember that Sunday night. That girl drove me over to Jacobi's and I picked up my card case. I called this morning and told all the places where I had charge plates that I had them back.

Tuesday night, while I was working, I had a phone call from the Operator. She said I was wanted in the Manager's office right away. You know me; right away, I thought I was going to be fired. Well, I went over, and I was told I am getting a raise and now I will be making $67 plus 1% commission. I was making $64 plus a 1% commission. It wasn't much, but I was proud of myself. He also told me I must be more aggressive and take the initiative more on my own. He says I have an extra girl every day from 9 to 2 and still, he sees me always tagging towels and rugs and always filling the counters while she is getting the customers. He says to tell her to bring the things out you want and fill those counters and then me take the customers. But I could never tell anyone what to do. I do all that and have 8 books to count once a month.

The" Case of the Falling Cans:" Ma always kept mundane things like shopping interesting.

December 10, 1967
Yesterday after work at 6 I went over to Acme to do my shopping. I just got started and was reaching up on the top shelf to get a couple of cans and the whole mess came down. One hit me on the corner of my eye and the other hit me and cut me on the arm. There must have been a dozen or more cans that hit the floor, and no one came to see what happened. Luckily my glasses weren't broken. Anyway, I went over to the office to report it. I told the manager and showed him where the cans hit me. He was not the least bit concerned, and he said, "OK, I'll go over and pick the cans up." He never asked me if I was hurt or how it happened. Believe me, if I had broken my glasses, he sure would have heard more, but I was relieved I wasn't hurt anymore. Of course, I will have a small shiner on the corner of my eye.

Trouble in the form of stress keeps coming to Ma's door figuratively. It never stops. I guess we will always be one of those multi-problem families, and Ma is the one who gets involved in some form regardless of the problem. Here is a typical example:

January 17, 1968
Danny. Pat and I all had the flu. Danny missed two days one week and two days this week, but he said he couldn't afford to take any more days off, what with having to pay Susie and me. But I said it would be better to take one whole week off at one time rather than to lose 2 or 3 weeks later. He was off Monday and Tuesday and today he came back. Around 1:30 today, he got a call from Susie that she had to take the two kids to the hospital because they didn't know which one had taken a whole bottle of baby Aspirin. Come to find out, it was Lisa. She ate them in the morning, and she didn't

find out about it until around noon time. The Doctor said that the pills had already gotten into her blood stream, but her system had digested the pills and she would be OK. When Danny and Susie left the hospital, they were feeding her intravenously.

A typical day for Ma at "The Refuge:" First, there was the night-time calamity related to the malfunctioning sump pump that Pat resolved; then the anxiety around Anne Marie's latest facial surgery; and finally, the exhilaration of Jill walking! Pat showed his uncanny problem-solving skills once again by fixing the sump pump!

January 27, 1968

When we were having that bitterly cold weather, the sump pump sprung a leak. I woke up one morning at about 5 and the old pump was going so loud, and I could hear water running so close. I knew it wasn't outside. I jumped out of bed and ran down to the cellar. The cap that connects the hose had worn almost through. There was water all over. I pulled the plug and Pat looked at it. He took the part with him and the man at the Hardware store said it would cost $6 or $7 to put a new one in, but to hold through the winter, he said he could solder the part. So, Pat had him do that for $35. That old pump is working just like new. If it goes next time, I'll have a new part put on.

I am trying to write this letter and Pat is sitting across from me figuring out his income and state tax. Occasionally, he starts talking to me, so if I seem to be jumping from one thing to another, you know what the trouble is.

Anne Marie had her operation, and although her face doesn't seem to be as bad as we all expected, the doctor said he had to go farther in than he expected. I was over there last Monday, and she still had her eye sewed shut. He had to cut into the Optic nerve. He said her eye will droop, but the good thing is nothing was malignant. That's what she and all of us were worried about.

Janice has about 4 weeks to go. She looks good, and she feels good. During the holidays, she put on a little more weight than the Doctor cared for, so she has gone back on her diet somewhat. Jill is walking all over. When Bernard came to Buffalo, that was the surprise they had for him. He is so crazy about her. She has been up here for 3 weeks, so she thinks Peter is her other Father. They are all coming for dinner tomorrow. I am going to have stew and dumplings.

Chapter 19

Ma's Health: Part II

Ma's legs are giving her more pain again if she is on her feet continuously. Without Ma having to beg Sears for an easier position, they offered her the opportunity to work in the Catalogue Department, where she could sit the whole time. She has mixed feelings about the transfer, but she knows this is the only way she can keep on working there. Somewhat of an additional benefit, her boss will be a good friend of mine who she has known for several years.

January 28, 1968
Yes, that was nice of Sears to do that for me. But it is a very boring job. Don't get me wrong. I am not complaining. But you sit all day just calling people and getting nothing; it gets very boring. Last Thursday and Friday, I must of called 150 people, and out of all those called, I sold $11.77 to one person. Of course, it is no reflection on me because these are new people I am calling, and they are either not interested, they come into the store and place their order, or they have another operator calling them. The only time you really make any money is when you are on incoming calls all day. That day, you don't call out at all, you just answer the bell. But I don't mind it; at least, as you say, I am off my feet.

The message in Ma's first sentence below could be the story of her life. Whatever mess or difficulty we each created, it all encroached on Ma's life. Her resilience was repeatedly tested, and how she coped with it all was remarkable.

February 4, 1968

We have had some more trouble. Last Thursday, Danny got a phone call, and it was to tell him that Susie was in Meyers. She had taken a bottle of antibiotic tablets. He got dressed and went right up there. They had pumped her stomach out and she will be there for the next 10 days. I just feel so bad for those poor kids. I said if I could do it, I would quit my job and take care of them (David and Lisa). They are so cute and self-reliant. So, Danny is there with the kids. He is working and has a young girl who stays there all day with the children. Susie is better but still in the hospital. I will let you know how she is from time to time.

February 20, 1968

How is everything over there? Everything is fine here. Susie comes home today, but she is still very nervous. I never got to see her, but Peter did. Tuesdays, he worked up there and he went to see her. He said he didn't wear his white coat because he thought it wouldn't look good to other patients.

Jimmy got hurt at work the other day. They thought at first his foot was broken, and he was looking forward to a six-week vacation, but it wasn't, thank goodness. He has badly bruised the tendons. He went back to work yesterday. This happened on Friday.

Pat and I are fine. He has a girlfriend, but I don't think it is anything serious. At least he doesn't act like it is.

Ma works her "interpersonal magic" to Pat's benefit!
February 27, 1968
Pat and I are fine. Great words for me to read and hear! *Sunday, he sold his record player. Yesterday, he called me at work to ask me to look at the stereos at the store. He intended to pay around $500 for one. Well, you know me, wheeling and dealing. I went right to the head one, who I know from working upstairs. He had a beautiful one, maple to match the furniture, and it was a floor model for*

146

$449.00. He took $50 off it for me. Of course, Pat came after work. I told him he didn't have to buy that one and for him to look at other ones. As soon as he saw it, he thought it was ideal, so he took it. One of the men I know has a station wagon. I called him and asked him if he would drive Pat, the stereo, and I home. We would pay him $5.

He said he would gladly drive us home, but no money. He said if he found any money on the seat, he would throw me and the stereo out in the snow. That is how kind the of people at the store are to me.

Ma is back home after a short hospital stay, but Pat brings another problem home!

April 11, 1968

Everything is going smoothly so far. My appetite is coming back slow but sure. I am feeling stronger all the time, but of course, not as before. I get sick every time I think of the pep I had before the operation; if only I had had that pep and my new legs, I could have done hundreds of other things. The doctors have said I will eventually, so I wait patiently. When I think of what I put your children through, I feel sick about it. Thank God it is all behind us now.

I was operated on 4 weeks ago yesterday and the children all told me I have come a long way and I guess I have. I stayed at Peter's from Thursday until Tuesday. Bernie and Anne Marie came that night. Anne Marie only stayed 3 days. Bernie came on Friday and took her home on Sunday. They kept saying they would come back if I wanted them to, but they planned on going to her Mother's for Easter and I didn't want them to upset their plans. Pat said he would help me with dishes and do the wash, so I figured we were all set. Monday, I cooked supper. Pat came from work and had his ring finger bandaged. An iron bar had fallen on the finger and cut the tip off past the nail. They rushed him to the Doctor. He put the tip back on and sewed it on. They just bandaged it, but the second joint is broken, and I guess today they will put a splint on it. He was shaking all over and in such terrible pain. Of course, I went to pieces and cried all over the place. I finally called Sue. Her and Jim came out. She did the dishes, and then we played some pinochle, which kind of helped Pat, too. The Doctor had given him some pain pills, but they never helped him. He was supposed to take 1 every 4 hours, but from 4:30 to 7 he had taken 5 with no relief, so when he went to bed, he took 2 pain pills and 2 of his own pills and he said he slept well. He said he was going to stop and buy a bottle of Guggenheim (whiskey) and drink the whole thing (joke). Now Kathleen is staying until Friday, and she is a big help to me and the company, too.

"Pat the Painter" and "Pat the Prom-Goer."
Mayb14, 1968
Last night, Pat came home and decided to start painting his room. So, he did the ceiling and tonight he is doing the walls. I have been trying to talk him into taking my bed and chifforobe, but he wants his own bed. I will make new curtains for him, and he will have his stereo and colored television in there, so I guess I'll see him for supper. But he does enjoy his stereo and I think it relaxes him.

On the 24th of May, Pat is taking Kathleen's girlfriend to the Senior Prom. They will go to the girl's house for cocktails and then to Kleinihan's Music Hall for the prom. The next day, the whole class goes to Chestnut Ridge Park for the Senior Picnic. He says that's pretty good; he is going to the Senior Prom, and he only went 6 weeks to high school. The afternoon of the Prom, Sue goes over to the school to pin one of the Roses on the Mothers and Kathleen asked me to come too. I am so happy about it.

Tears for different reasons are below. Very poignant images:
June 2, 1968
A week ago, Friday, I went with Sue and Kathleen to Senior Day at South Park. Sue and I had a crying good time. Sue for memories,

me, because I'm afraid Kathleen will probably be the only grandchild I will see graduate from High School. They served cookies and lemonade down in the cafeteria afterward.

Ma's doctor tells it like it is, and she gets it!
June 4, 1968
I didn't want to finish this letter until I went to see Dr. Yerkovich. Today, I went and he told me that if they had waited two more months, I would have lost both of my legs because gangrene had already set in. That's why I haven't been able to walk outside. I can walk in the house and up and down stairs, but today, he said he said I should try my legs. So tomorrow, if the weather stays nice (it's supposed to go to 80 degrees), I will go out and try walking. When I think what could of happened, I really get scared.

More good news from Ma's doctor: "He is in awe of me!"
August 7, 1968
Yesterday, Sue took me to Dr. Yerkovich, and he was really pleased with my progress. I told Sue he seems to, always since my operation, look at me in awe. More than once, he has said it is a miracle I am here and that he can hardly believe it is me. He also told me to do some walking to exercise my legs. I asked him if there is a chance of this recurring on me, and he said no, that I had good openings now with the plastic tubing in my legs. I don't have to see Dr. Alfano (her surgeon) now until January.

Just the kind of day Ma absolutely loves!
August 13, 1968
Saturday, Jim, Pat, and Peter painted the living room. Sue and Jim came on Friday night and stayed overnight. Pat came from work and said he had to work Saturday for a few hours. So, Jim started painting about 9:30 A.M. Sue and I went and did grocery shopping. Peter came out, but he had so many patients to write up on and so much studying to do that maybe Janice would drive out herself (Did I tell you that the baby is 5 months old now and creeping soldier

149

style on his stomach?). So about 2:00 o'clock came Peter in his painting clothes with his own brush, roller and pan. About 10 minutes later, in drives Bernard and Anne Marie, and then at 3 Pat called and said he was on his way home. For supper, I had Jim, Sue, Shawn, Peter, and Janice, the baby, Bernard, Anne Marie, Jill, Pat, and myself. It was a good thing that Sue and I had decided to cook a big roast that night and have spaghetti Sunday night.

Pat recruits a handy neighbor to save the day and beyond for Ma! This is an example of Pat's growing confidence.

September 7, 1968

Last Saturday, the washer broke down and I was fit to be tied. With me going back to work, I knew there would be no one home all day to have Sears come and look at it and they don't work on Saturdays. I was really in a dither. Right in the middle of washing, too! So, Pat went down the street to this Danny DeMarco. He came right over and had it going again in about 5 minutes. So, while he was here, I had him put new washers in the bathroom sink and tub. The whole job cost me $4.50. We still must get larger washers for the bathroom because the ones we had were not quite the size, so he said if I get the bigger ones, he will put them on for free.

Sears welcomes Ma back!

September 10, 1968

Today, I was back at work for 1 week. It seems good to be back. Everyone was so glad to see me. The first couple of days, I never had so many hugs and kisses from people. They were genuinely concerned. I never knew I was so well-liked and missed.

Pat takes an important step in his future:

September 12, 968

Pat got his brochure on the High School Equivalency preparation course. They have one at Southside Junior High School. That is on Bailey Avenue, just above where Sue used to live on Kimmel

Avenue. I am glad he is going to start, and he is anxious (eager, not nervous) about it too.

Happy Birthday to the handiest guy in "The Refuge."
October 2, 1968
Pat is getting so darn handy. The faucet in the bathroom sink was leaking terribly and the toilet was also leaking. It just never shut off. So, I bought some new washers, and he stopped off at Woepples hardware store and asked the man in there about how to fix it. The fellow explained how to do it. So, on Sunday, he fixed the faucet and in about 1 hour, he had the toilet all fixed. So that saved me a considerable amount of money there. Those plumbers charge just to step inside your door. Now I want to buy two new stationery wash tubs, so if I do, I'm sure Pat can connect them up. You see, that one tub has a hole in it. Because of that time, Bernard put a keg of beer into the tub and it split the tub. I only have to buy one, but I wouldn't be able to match it with the other in color.

Pat had a nice birthday. Sue and Jim gave him a nice permanent-press shirt, a sort of gold color. Peter, Janice, Danny, Susie, Bernard, Anne Marie, and I chipped in $3 and bought him a nice record cabinet with the same wood grain as his stereo, walnut. Janice had a big, wide pink ribbon tied around it and a big pink and silver bow. When Peter brought it out to show him after supper, we didn't know if he was going to laugh or cry or have a seizure. He said he never expected anything like that. It was Peter's idea and I thought it was a good one.

Good news and bad news for Pat in the next letter, and he loses and finds his wallet in the letter after that!

October 26, 1968
Last night Pat went to the nose Doctor. His breathing had gotten so bad he was having a hard time eating and breathing. The Doctor said he has an infection in the nose right now, so he must put 5

151

drops of this medicine in each nostril for 2 weeks and then go back. He will be operated on the first part of December. We don't know the exact date, but I will let you know. He will feel better once he can breathe properly.

October 28, 1968
Saturday night Pat went to the show with Sue and Jim. When they came out, they went to have a drink. Pat reached for his wallet, and it was gone. They drove back to the show, but it was closed. Sunday morning, Bernard drove him up to the show and the owner let them in. There the wallet was, it was down in the seat. Was he ever glad? So was I.

Ma gets a scare!
November 7, 1968
Remember I told you I had my flu shot? Well, I did catch a cold and it settled in my head, but I thought it was all clearing up. About a week ago, my right ear felt like it wanted to pop; it felt like there was a lot of wax in it. I also have a little headache. But you know me; I diagnosed the case as a lot of wax in the ear. Yesterday, on my way to the Emergency Room. I thought, here I go again, back in the old hospital for 4 or 6 weeks. But thank goodness I didn't have to. The Doctor told me I had a minor case of the flu, and it settled in my right ear. Consequently, my equilibrium was off balance. He told me to stay home the rest of the week. I am taking penicillin and drops it in my ears. If it didn't clear up in 24 hours, he would have to open the ear. It feels better today, and I hope it stays that way.

Pummeling at its finest! Terrible!
December 3, 1968
Pat asked Peter if he was going to come to see him in the hospital, and Peter said, "Hell no, because when I leave, you will scream and holler and want to go home too." Pat bought a Swinger camera, and he has been having a ball. He has more pictures of me than anything or anyone else. It will be nice for Christmas, though, when

the whole family is here Christmas Eve. I can hardly believe that Christmas is only 21 days away. No snow, but cold.

Some nose surgery for Pat:

December 16, 1968

Pat went into the hospital Tuesday afternoon, was operated on Wednesday morning, came home Thursday, and went back to work today. He feels good, but the Doctor said it will be a couple of weeks before he can feel a difference in his breathing because his nose is still swollen inside. But he sure sounds different sleeping. Better.

Good times and good medical news for Ma:

January 14, 1969

I have started my part-time job and love it. The first 3 days, I come home, take a nap, then get up and do whatever has to be done, and get supper. It feels good to be able to have supper on the stove ready to serve Pat. When I was working full-time, we never ate until after 7 o'clock.

On January 6th, I went to see Dr. Alfano, the surgeon. He said I was doing good. Then he asked me to show him my heels because the last time he saw my heels, they were an odd color. So, when he saw them, he said they had a good color now. Peter said why didn't I tell him I took a bath. (joke)

Ma implicitly expresses a desire to live to age 70 and reminisces about long ago Christmases when her family had wealth and she lived in what at that time was considered a mansion (the "Big House") in those days.

January 20, 1969

Say, I would like to try for 70!! How about it?

You spoke of the Christmas tree with the candles. Do you remember the two Christmas trees we had at the big house? We always had a big one and then the one we had in the parlor that held candles.

When I was a little girl, my Mother used to take the little tree out in the kitchen and light the candles, but she would leave them lit only for a few minutes. I don't remember if she ever lit them when you and Susan were small. When you mentioned the tree, it brought back some memories.

BINGO!

Pat and I were finished with supper and we both had our pajamas on. He was all set to go to bed and read the paper. I was all set to watch TV and relax for the evening. Pat called Sue to ask her if he could come for supper tomorrow night. She said yes and that tonight her and Jimmy were going to Bingo. Pat and I got ready in 10 minutes, called a cab, and were in there in about 20 minutes. No one won, but we had some good laughs.

Pat takes a "Staycation," and Ma worries, sort of. It is great that Pat has a job and can afford to enjoy life!

February 10, 1969
Pat has been on vacation, and he still has another week to go. He was going to go to Chicago or New York or Washington. But he decided to stay home and buy himself some clothes. Now, he is waiting for his Income Tax check. He spends money like it was going out of style, but after all, he doesn't have a family to support. I told him he should put at least $5 per week in the bank, but he doesn't believe it, so I left him alone. If he pays his board, there isn't much else I can do.

If the opportunity presents itself, Ma is ready to drive again. All she needs is a car! She loved the car that I wrecked and will never forgive myself. It gave her the independence and convenience she never had because this was the first car in our family.

February 24, 1969
I finally had my Driver's license renewed. Not that I am expecting to drive, but more for identification. Besides, as Sue says, who knows when there might be an emergency sometime. I thought I had a lot of time when you said I had a year to renew it. At that time, a year seemed a long way off. Suddenly, I decided I didn't have that much time to spare. I got my license!

Pat surprises Ma with a thrilling gift!
March 6, 1969
Last Monday, Pat went over to the new Seneca Mall they built here in West Seneca. He came home about 9:30 P.M. He walked in and said, "Ma, I bought you something tonight." I couldn't imagine what it could be, and he bought me a G.E. dishwasher. It is beautiful. It is a portable one. I got it Wednesday, so I had saved all my dirty dishes for 3 days and the two of us put it to work that night. It does a good job. There aren't enough dishes from us from one night, so I just save them, put them in the dishwasher, close it down (not tight) and my shelf is always clean.

Ma really does love a houseful mixed with a little drama! A great day!
March 10, 1969
Yesterday, I had the family out. Sue says I just love a crowd and I'm not happy unless I have a crowd around me. There was Patrick, me, Sue, Jim, Shawn, Wasson, Peter, Janice, Peter, Jr., Danny, David, and Lisa. Kathleen and Ray were supposed to come too, but she doesn't like a crowd. Susie didn't come because her and Danny are separated. Danny has a room near his work. It is a long story, but believe me, it is for the best. I will explain it all when you come home. He has visitation rights on the weekends. Getting back to yesterday, the girls were dying to use the dishwasher, and it sure got a workout. We put the dishes in, closed it up, turned it on and we sat down and played Michigan Rummy.

Fridays are Ma's and Sue's special day.

April 25, 1969

Every Friday lately, Sue and I seem to be together all day. We go and get our hair done once a week at 11:00 A.M., go over to Sears to get my pay, go shopping, come back here to my house, I put my meat away, and then we go into her house, put her groceries away, and I stay there for supper and then we go to Bingo. She said to Jim, by the time Bingo is over, it's time to take my Mother home. Of course, she is only kidding (I think?).

Another milestone for Ma!

May 6, 1969

We are all well here. Sunday, Sue, Jim, Shawn, Kathleen, Ray, Peter, Janice, baby Peter, and Danny were out for dinner. We celebrated Janice's birthday. Sue made an announcement. Kathleen is expecting a baby in November. Sue will be a grandmother and I will be a great-grandmother. Kathleen has been very sick, but not like Sue was anyway.

Ma has a way of saying extraordinary things in such a matter-of-fact way. I guess change is the way of life, especially Ma's.

May 7, 1969

Danny quit his job and he might go back to the Navy. Pat came home from work and told me. I called him later in the evening and he said he has to go back uptown to the Post Office building tomorrow to find out about the Navy and then he will let me know. One boy coming out and one boy going in.

Chapter 20

A Major Change for Pat and Ma

At Ma's request, "The Refuge" house has been sold, and Ma and Pat are now renting a second-floor flat back in South Buffalo. The decision to sell "The Refuge" was not one that 100% of the family supported, but it certainly was beneficial to both Ma and Pat in several ways. Maybe the biggest benefit is that the move put Ma and her "best buddy," Sue, within five minutes of each other. If Ma needed anything, Sue could get to her so much quicker than she could with the trek to "The Refuge." Also, they enjoy each other so much that their new proximity will facilitate many more contacts for just socialization, which they both love. Another advantage to the move is that Pat's ability to get to work is so much easier. He now has co-workers that he may be able to ride with, and there are far more frequent buses available if he needs them. I think also that Pat and Ma appreciate not having to worry about the day-to-day maintenance of "The Refuge." Now, if something breaks, all they have to do is call the owner. This is a big relief for both Pat and Ma.

Despite these benefits, there are downsides to the move. Ma loses out on her co-workers who gave her rides to and from Sears because they do not live in South Buffalo, nor does anyone else. She is now entirely dependent on the bus system for getting to and from work. Another major downside is the number of floors in this residence and the age of the homes in comparison. "The Refuge" was a ranch-style home on one floor with everything new, and the flat is an older two-story home that needs work. Stairs were always a real problem for Ma, and now she must negotiate two stories. Then, after Ma and Pat moved in, they realized that there were very few screens for the windows, and the water pressure was extremely poor, making bathing an ordeal. Regardless of these deficits, Ma and Pat decided to make a move back to our beloved South Buffalo.

Note: Below is the last letter from Ma in 1970 until the one below, dated March 12, 1970. This was due to Tommy's retirement from the Air Force and his return to the U.S.A. in the summer of 1969. He and his family moved to California, and Ma is preparing to fly for the first time in her life to go visit them.

The letter right below is from Uncle Wasson (Ma's only sibling) to Tommy and Karoline. The subsequent letters were from Ma.

March 3, 1970
Dear Tommy, Karoline, and Thea,

Just dropping you and the family a little line. I haven't heard from you in quite a while. How is everything out there? Anyway, you don't have to worry about shoveling snow.

Your Mother was saying that you were building a house. How is it coming along? She also said you were very busy between building the new house and your position.

I haven't seen much of the family lately, but have talked to Janice, Peter, and your Mother.

When the weather breaks a little and gets warmer, I will have to take a bus ride out to see Sue, your Mother, Peter and Janice, and, of course, Peter, Jr.

I took out Medicare and they take $5.50 a month out of my Social Security check a month.

So, I am sending you a Money Order for $20.00 for payment on the TV set, which is working very well.

There isn't much else to say now. So, take care of yourself and give my regards to Karoline and Thea.

I will close as of now.

Good Luck,
Wasson

This is an unusually short letter for Ma. She was not feeling well at this time, and we hope her next doctor' appointment will provide some direction to help her.

March 12, 1970

How is everything and everyone there? We are all fine here, yes, even me. There isn't much to tell you, because I don't go to the Doctor until the 17ᵗʰ of March. Peter has called the Doctor and he said they are going to see how I am when I come in for my check-up. They don't want to operate if they don't have to.

The trouble with me is that I have a lot of ambition but nowhere to put it.

Are you all moved out to Livermore yet? Did you have to pay 2 months' rent? Does Karoline feel any better? I worry about you people out there. If only there was something I could do.

Pat does my shopping and washing. I just sit and rest all day, and I try to keep myself busy crocheting and doing number paintings.

Ma seems to have bounced back and is as busy as ever, but she also seems to know her limits (really?).

April 6, 1970

Last week, I was a busy grandmother and great-grandmother. Kathleen finally found a place to move to. So she was busy getting the place in order, scrubbing and cleaning, so Thursday, I went to Susan's and babysat Christopher, got supper and made a cake. Friday, they brought him here and I took care of him. Sue came for supper, later Peter came and picked me up and I babysat Peter, Jr. and Jill. Jill came and stayed at Peter's for a week. Janice was going to stand up for a wedding and she had to go to practice that night. After the rehearsal, Peter went over to the house for a party.

Saturday was the wedding, so I had the two kids all day and evening. Bernard had to play Saturday night, so he came in around 5 and helped me put the two kids to bed. He took me home Sunday morning. I said no babysitting next week. I am taking a week off. While I was at Peter's, Pat called me on Saturday to say Danny was back in town and was staying at our flat.

Ma's surgeon wants her to walk but with moderation. Like many of us Taltys, we don't know what "moderation" means, and the excerpt below proves this in Ma's case:

April 7, 1970

Dr. Alfano said I should walk but not too far at once, so yesterday, I ventured out. I took my Income Tax check and my check from Sears and cashed them at the bank, then I went to the South Side Furniture store and bought a base cabinet for my kitchen to set beside my sink. Then I went to the 5 & 10 store and bought some yarn to make myself a vest, and then I went to the A & P and got a few groceries. I felt good, of course; my leg got bad, but I just stood and looked in the windows and window-shopped until I could get going again. I was gone 2 hours, which should have only been walking for half or three-quarters of an hour.

I tell you, it is terrible to be like this. I just can't get used to being closed in like this. Sue said I always tried to do too much in one day anyway, so I guess now I must pay for that.

Ma has had to adjust her routines, but she cannot resist an opportunity to see one of her grandbabies:

April 19, 1970

Last Wednesday, I was sitting down in the cellar washing (that's what I do on wash days). Pat carries the box of clothes down and when I finish the wash, I fold everything and pack the box and he brings it back upstairs when he comes home. Anyway, I was washing, and Bernard came in from Rochester and asked me if I wanted to go back with him until Saturday when he had to come in

160

to play in a band. Besides, he wanted me to see the baby. So, I finished the wash, and he came back and picked me up about 3.

Sadness and worries keep creeping into Ma's life. Sadly, there are just no respites for her.

April 23, 1970

Bob Goodwin called me today to tell me that his Father passed away this morning. He wanted me to call Bernard and tell him. When Bernard came in last Saturday, he went over to the hospital to see him. I guess he got pretty shook up because first, Mr. Goodwin looked so terrible and 2nd, he was in the same ward where Dad was. Dad will be gone 7 years from tomorrow. I have a Memoriam in tomorrow's newspaper. (Ma always kept track of everyone's birthdays and death days).

I told you on the phone that Danny was staying with me. He was going to leave to go back to Washington next week, but I think he has changed his mind. At least, I hope so. I don't ask him anything. You know how close-mouthed he is. I talk when he decides to tell me something. Anyway, the other day, he said why don't I call Susie and talk to her? I had wanted to but didn't think I should. So, I called her, and she said that David can't go to school anymore. The Principal sent him home with a note saying not to send him back because he could not cooperate with the teachers or his classmates. So, when Danny came home from work, I told him and said that child loves you, so how can you go away and leave him? Last night, he went out and waited for Susie to come from work. He didn't come home last night and tonight he is going to meet her again and talk. So, I don't know what is going to happen. I will let you know in the next letter about the next chapter.

Ma adapts to not having window screens throughout the flat and amazes Pat!

April 29, 1970

In the meantime, I was dying with no breeze, and you know me. So yesterday, I went to the store and bought curtain material, which is a closer weave than netting (39 cents a yard remnant). I cut the material to fit the windows and the ones that don't have any screens, for I tacked all the way around. Now, I can open and close the windows with no fear of flies or mosquitoes. Pat thinks I am "the most." He kept looking at the windows and saying, "Boy, that is something I would have never thought of that." Now, when I find out how many screens I have (I don't know that yet), I will do the same to those who don't have any. When Peter called last night, Pat told him and Peter couldn't figure out how I did it. Ma's landlord *said he was going to get her some aluminum storms and screens for some of my windows, but he and his wife took a week off and went to Florida, so I guess that's where my screens and storms went.*

Ma gets some ominous news from an unexpected source:

May 5, 1970

Today, I went to the foot Doctor. I'm trying to get myself put back together for when I go back to work. Anyway, the foot Doctor said he hadn't seen me since November and wanted to know what I had been doing. I told him I had been to California and in the hospital. I told him why and then I asked him if he was still contemplating operating on me. He said, "I should say not; I wouldn't touch you now, not with your poor circulation."

Ma gets some good news regarding transportation to work:

May 20, 1970

Today, I went to work. It was tough just getting from home to the bus. I sat on the fence on Indian Church Road for a few minutes, then stood in front of Berst's for a few minutes, crossed the street and sat on the newspaper box until the bus came. Everyone was glad to see me at work, and it felt good to come back. One of the

162

new girls spoke up and asked me if I would change my hours. She would pick me up and bring me home. So, after today, I will be working from 10-3.

The story below was about one-time trouble that literally did come to Ma's door:

July 7, 1970

The other night, I was just finishing up my dishes and the girl downstairs rapped on my back door. She said there were two men in their house that wanted to see me. I asked her why they hadn't come upstairs, and she said that, evidently, my bell didn't ring, and they rang their bell. You can imagine what was going through my head. Anyway, I went down there. It was two plainclothes men and they wanted to know where Danny was and where Susie was. I told them I didn't know. They said that they had been told that Danny, Susie, and the children had moved in with me. I said no, that only Danny had, and he had left about 6 weeks ago, and I hadn't heard anything from him. They said they wanted him for non-support. Sue said she thinks they want him for something else besides that. They finally left and I asked my landlord how to come. They came to his house. He said that they had rung my bell and then his. When he answered the door, they told him they were looking for me and Mr. Furlong thought it would be best if they brought me down there. But if there was any trouble, he just as soon not has them see me, that he would get in touch with one of my children, because I have a bad heart and he knew I couldn't take it. I thought that was very nice of him, don't you?

The limitations that Ma is living with are making her life very difficult!

July 21, 1970

The last two days, I have had to take the bus to and from work. In the morning, it is bad for me because I am busy before I leave, taking a bath, getting dressed, and making the bed, and it really is tough on the leg when I start working. My bus comes at 9:04 and I leave the house at 8:30 to get to Seneca Street. Coming home isn't bad because I am sitting on the bus riding home, so I can walk OK. This drives me crazy. I have so much ambition bottled up inside of me and I can't do a thing.

Note: Sadly, the above was Ma's last letter. She died at home on August 4, 1970, after suffering another heart attack. Rest well, Ma! You deserve it!

"I have fought a good fight. I have finished my course; I have kept the faith."
The second Epistle of Paul to Timothy

The death of Ma was the worst thing to happen to all of us. She was a major force in all our lives. It was an awful shock. Now, Pat would be all alone. What will he do? Where will he go to live (he cannot afford the flat)? Will he survive? I was very worried about him.

Chapter 21

Pat's Life Without Ma

Moving on without Ma for me was very difficult. Recalling the abrupt and terrible way Ma was taken from us is still so very hard to think about. Even today, over 53 years later, I can cry when I think of Ma's difficult life and sudden death. I know it was devastating for us all, but I think even more so for Pat. Why? Simple math. My brothers and sister all had spouses and kids to love and to be loved by. All Pat had was Ma. I know he loved us, his siblings, but he really had only Ma. He never had a girlfriend or a special friend; Ma was it. She loved him unconditionally. This was evident in her letters regardless of what he did or didn't do. This is not to say that she did not express anger and frustration at times when his behavior defied logic, but at the root of it all, she loved Pat unconditionally.

Yes, it is expected that all parents will love their children unconditionally, but clinical psychologist Carl Rogers incorporated this thinking into his classic theory of psychotherapy, where the therapist views his or her client with what Rogers refers to as: "*unconditional positive regard.*" He explained that unconditional means "No conditions of acceptance...It is at the opposite pole from a selective evaluating attitude." He wrote that *positive* means "*A warm acceptance of the person. A genuine caring for the client.*" (or offspring). This description is not to imply that Ma was acting as Pat's therapist. It is just to show a parallel kind of caring that mirrored the way she cared about Pat for all his life. She was his *protective factor.*

So, what happened to Pat, who lost the only person on earth that cared about him so much? Surprisingly, he carried on. He went to work every day. Paid his bills. Watched his favorite TV shows. Took care of the things he valued. Listened to his music. Helped us clean out Ma's stuff. I strongly belief my sister Sue and her husband Jim were the ones who sustained him during the initial phases of his grief.

Speaking of Sue and Jim, they did the most remarkable thing when they invited Pat to move in with them! They did this twice before for our whole family. How could they? Why would they? Regardless, they took Pat home with them from the hospital after a quick stop at Ma's to pick up some clothes and stuff. The next time he went back to the flat, it was to help us clean it out.

Pat enjoyed a period of stability and tranquility, and then things fell apart. It began with an accident on the job. He had a seizure while driving his Towmotor and drove it off the dock. Incredibly, he was not seriously injured, but for safety reasons, he lost his job. The Union supported Pat's grievance that he was discriminated against by the Company because of his disability (epilepsy). His case went before the local NLB (National Labor Relations Board) and Pat lost. He lost his case, and he lost the best job he ever had. Also, the prospects of finding another were bleak now that his seizures and the accident were a part of his permanent record of employment. It was also the end of the most productive and happiest days of his life.

He was miserable as he went back on the all too familiar search for another job. He also made no effort to hide his misery, nor would he help with chores at Sue and Jim's. Sue knew it was time for Pat to go when she noticed Jim folding Pat's laundry while Pat relaxed and watched TV.

However, she knew she did not have the emotional strength to ask him to leave. So, she asked my brother Bernie to do it, and he did. A few days later, Bernie asked Pat if he wanted to go out and have a beer with him. After a few beers, Bernie gave Pat the bad news. This "eviction notice" was, of course, perceived by Pat in a negative way. Another pummeling? Of course!

Fortuitously, just a few houses from where I lived with my family on Buffalo's Westside, friends of my wife had an apartment for rent. I brought Pat to see it, and he took it. Now, the question was, how would he pay for it when his Unemployment ran out? Around this time, Pat began researching the possibility of his going on SSI (Social Security Disability Insurance). From what I could understand, Pat would qualify for it. He applied and after several weeks of anxious waiting, he was approved. He was also automatically enrolled in Medicare, and that would cover his increasingly expensive medicines and other medical expenses. He was very happy in his new apartment and with a steady income and health insurance through Medicare. So, some of his most immediate problems were resolved.

I liked having Pat near me, but not living with me because of his moodiness. I could take him shopping and he had dinner with us once or twice a week. We let him do his laundry at our place, and he helped me out with projects around the house. Also, often on Fridays, Pat and I would go "drinking and drugging" with our brother Danny. Those were crazy nights!

Another positive thing about Pat living just down the street was that our son, Peter, Jr was three years old, and he loved visiting his Uncle Pat's place and sometimes sleeping over at his apartment. Pat loved it also. We thought Pat had the ideal set-up, but after a short time, it seemed he found something better.

He learned that they were building a new apartment complex just behind City Hall and Pat's status of living on SSI would qualify him for one of the apartments. They expected to have them completed within a year. His rent would be cheaper, and everything would be brand new. I thought it was a chance for him to move up. In a few months, his application was approved, and he began packing up for the move to the Pine Harbor Apartments. Here is a description of the new complex that they used to promote it:

Welcome Home to Pine Harbor Apartments, a Downtown Buffalo community combining extraordinary convenience and affordable, spacious living. Surrounded by a park-like setting of mature trees, Pine Harbor is just minutes from shopping, restaurants, recreation areas, lively entertainment and maintains easy access to surrounding Interstates. Pine Harbor offers a variety of spacious 1-, 2-, 3- & 4-bedroom apartment homes as well as 4-bedroom town homes designed for your comfort and with all utilities included. Call or stop in today to find out why Pine Harbor is the perfect choice to call home for you and your family!

Then, things changed. Soon after Pat moved into Pine Harbor, I had an opportunity for a promotion, but it would require our moving to Syracuse, NY, about three hours away. I took the position and off we went to Syracuse, where we lived for three years (1974 – 1977). During that time, Pat stayed with us for long weekends, which we all enjoyed. He also had made some friends (finally!) at Pine Harbor who could take him shopping or just hang out in each other's apartments listening to music.

To support a statement I made earlier that neither Pat nor I were racists like our Dad, Pat became a part of a black social group of people in Pine Harbor and they facilitated his becoming accepted by a larger group of black people who socialized at a tavern in the inner city. Pat enjoyed spending time with all of them, but especially one older woman ("Mabel Jean") who did a lot for Pat.

168

When I first met Mabel Jean, I was confused. Was Mabel Jean his girlfriend or his substitute mother? She was older than Pat by about twenty years, and she was overly solicitous in terms of caring for Pat, cooking for him, and reassuring him when he was upset. Regardless of the arrangement, it was working for both. Of course, I can imagine our Dad doing three flips in his grave when he heard about Pat's unusual relationship with Mabel Jean and the black social group that he joined.

We were in Syracuse for just over three years when I was able to return to the Buffalo area and take a joint position at the University at Buffalo as a Clinical Professor of Occupational Therapy and as the Director of OT at the Erie County Medical Center. These were exciting times for the whole family because we missed everybody, and they missed us. We bought a house in Tonawanda on the same street as my brother Bernie and his wife Anne Marie, who was also my wife's sister. However, I had a dilemma. Both of my future bosses wanted me on the job as soon as possible, but we had a house to sell back in Syracuse, and we wouldn't be able to occupy our new house for a month. Solution? Stay with Pat?

I assumed that because of all the favors I had done for Pat over the years, especially those years when we lived on the same block, I could now cash in. I was wrong. Why was he silent when I asked if I could put a cot up in his one bedroom for about 30 days? Also, why the glum face? After a few minutes of eerie silence, it came: "Sometimes Mabel Jean stays over." So, that's it? Time to wheel and deal.

"How about this for a plan? I stay here Monday through Thursday, and she can stay over Friday through Sunday. It's only for a month. What do you think?"

"We don't like no schedules. When the time is right, we just do it! You'll have to go someplace else."

So, I silently raged to myself. Past favors meant nothing? I could see that laying on some guilt was not going to work with this guy. Let's see if he is still as mercenary as he was in the past. "What about twenty bucks a night for Monday through Thursday? That's 80 bucks that I really can't afford, but I have no place else to go." More silence. I can out-silence him. Maybe.

It worked! "It's okay if you stay here on those nights you said. You don't have to pay me anything. I'll just tell Mabel Jean that some nights, she'll have to wait a day or two for her sugar." Wow! What a response! What an image! 300 pounds of Pat wrestling around with Mabel Jean in his single bed! That was not anything I wanted to witness!

Chapter 22

ACEs and Pat as a Single Middle-aged Adult

(Counter-ACEs Leading to Resilience)

After spending all those evenings and nights in January, I realized that Pat had changed during the three years I was in Syracuse, but I surely did not know the extent of the changes. However, over three or four years of interacting with him while drinking and drugging with our brother Danny, I got to see and hear the changes first-hand. Apparently, the time spent in the Pine Harbor Apartments was a respite from the pummelings that had been the hallmark of Pat's life.

I now saw a different Pat in the ways he interacted with his friends from the community, his Pine Harbor neighbors who would stop by unannounced to visit and hear him on the phone. He was now more outgoing and friendly, and I cannot believe I'm saying this, but he was approaching suave, charming, and even cool, all at rudimentary levels, of course. Prior to this epiphany, I would have described Pat as a sullen, morose, and angry person. He was this way with Danny and me, but he switched when interacting with his newly found friends. I then saw what he was doing. He was, in the language of the ACEs study, unknowingly developing *Counter-ACEs leading to resilience*. Although at the age of 31, he was doing what most people do much earlier in life, he really was developing resilience, which was a great defense to any pummeling that may come his way. This is what the ACE literature refers to as the *very important individual, family, and community conditions that can support or build resilience using these protective factors*:

- Close relationships with competent or caring adults. I saw Mabel Jean doing this with her solicitousness (anxious concern and caring for "someone"), and that "someone" would be Pat.

- Identifying and cultivating a sense of purpose (faith, culture, identity) - Mabel Jean took Pat to her church and to a tavern where he connected with and identified with a small group of black people.

- Individual developmental competencies (problem-solving skills, self-regulation, agency) – Pat had grown in each of these areas, but his sense of agency was where I saw the greatest change. The sense of agency, or sense of control, is the subjective awareness of initiating, executing, and controlling one's own volitional actions in the world. It is the pre-reflective awareness or implicit sense that it is I who is executing bodily movement or thinking thoughts. Wikipedia. He would no longer be the pummeled punching bag. It seems Pat's participation in Project Pathway, plus whatever he picked up from interacting with his new friends, gave him the rudiments of these skills, and now he was unintentionally busy honing them.

- Social connections and communities and social systems that support health and development and nurture social capital – I think this got started in the Pine Harbor Apartments and expanded further through Mabel Jean's many relationships. Certainly, these people are stronger in the social systems than they are in the supportive health aspects. Most of them smoked, all of them drank, and there was minimal concern about the foods they ate or how much they weighed.

I do not think that Pat developing the above **protective factors** later in life at 31 years of age would have the same benefits that a younger person before age 18 would have, but the research on this aspect of ACEs is limited. He has found quite an ally, advocate, model, and guide in Mabel Jean. To me, she is over-solicitous, but Pat loves her caring and guiding nature. Is Mabel Jean a substitute for Ma? Freud would say yes, but I think it's simply a mutually beneficial relationship. She needs someone who needs and appreciates her, and Pat fits both.

I had many opportunities to observe the "new Pat" in action when he, Danny, and I would go out on too many Friday nights drinking and drugging. During this time, I also bought a pool table and built a recreation room and bar in our basement because we all loved to shoot pool. We also liked to gamble a little bit and thus played 9-Ball a lot. Danny has two daughters who were around my daughter Beth's age, and they enjoyed getting together and doing whatever ten to twelve-year-old girls do.

So, on many Sundays, I would pick up Danny and the girls and then pick up Pat, and we would spend a pleasant afternoon playing pool, and then have a great dinner that Janice would put together, and sometimes have a cookout. I would then take them all back home.

Interestingly, on these Friday nights and Sunday afternoons, Pat would return to his old behaviors. I guess the changes that I witnessed when Pat interacted with his new friends were not as permanent as I thought. The change in his behavior seemed to be dictated by the people around him. I found this disappointing. He would return to his sullen and morose ways, which were annoying. Also, he and Danny were never close and produced some friction until we got high or drunk.

Then, on July 25, 1982, I was the one that changed. It was on that date that "I saw the light" and quit drinking and drugging. A year or two later, all my brothers were also clean and sober. Danny and Pat achieved sobriety through AA and NA, whereas I achieved mine

173

through my work as an occupational therapist working in an inpatient substance abuse treatment center. The three of us became different people, and most certainly for the better. I think Pat became mentally sharper. He became more astute at reading people. When he would share his insights about someone, they were surprisingly exact, intuitive, and often funny as hell.

Chapter 23

Pat Makes a Downward Change in Residences

I was somewhat shocked to find out that after eight happy years at the Pine Harbor Apartments, Pat moved into a somewhat dilapidated area of the city and into a hovel of a flat over a tavern. It usually doesn't work out too well for a person in recovery from alcoholism to take up residence directly over a place where alcohol is served. There is a crude but relevant saying in AA that "you can take a priest to a whorehouse only so many times before he drops his pants." Yes, it is crude, but it makes the point in a profound way. The building itself was in a state of general neglect and disrepair. The flat needed a good cleaning, which did not happen prior to Pat moving in two months ago. How this downward trek came about is a story in itself.

Apparently, there had been repeated increases in the rent at Pine Harbor that were greater than Pat's SSI monthly check. In addition to that, his seizure medication has been changed to one that was not covered under Medicare. So, he was looking for a cheaper place to live when some friends of his took him to this tavern below the flat he now rents. He had such a good time at the tavern that he went back several times and got to know some of the other patrons and the owner.

Then, one fateful night, he was enjoying himself with his new friends at the tavern when he asked if anyone knew of a cheap place that he could rent. Someone said that Dick, who owned the tavern as well as the building, was looking for someone to rent the second-floor flat. They also said that the flat is in tough shape. Pat then asked Dick about the flat, and apparently, the rent was far cheaper than what he was paying at the Pine Harbor Apartments.

Evidently, when it comes to a place to live, Pat was focused only on the cost per month. Such things as appearance, location, neighborhood, convenience, safety, security, cleanliness, a working stove, ventilation, and so forth were of little concern. He also wanted to get a dog, and the landlord was fine with that.

The shock that I experienced when I heard he was leaving Pine Harbor paled in comparison to the shock I felt when I saw this place for the first time. Because he was fine with it, and I didn't have to live there, I just said, "If this works for you, then it's fine with me." (I just hated going there).

My brothers and I helped him move in, but not with any sort of excitement. Because we could see he was going from a nice apartment, only eight years old and modern, to a decrepit flat in a house about 60 years-old and into what seemed a less safe neighborhood.

Fortunately, our assessment of the neighborhood was not accurate. It was a working-class collection of neighbors who had resided in their homes for many, many years and were happy there. The ones I talked with didn't see it as unsafe as I did, and their information was based on living there.

Most of the time, Pat was able to maintain his sobriety by just drinking Pepsi each time he stopped in the tavern. He enjoyed the people who came in there each night and, especially, the nights when spontaneous sing-alongs took place. One of Pat's gifts was the ability to imitate some of the patrons singing, and it was very funny as he sang in different voices for us.

Pat got his puppy and named him Dino (after Dean Martin, for some reason). He turned out to be a great dog. He was smart, friendly, and loved to play and run around the big backyard and in the big flat with few furnishings that they had all to themselves. Being a handy guy, Pat built Dino a very fine and secure doghouse where Pat could leave him outside all day if Pat was going to be gone shopping or to doctors' appointments. They were both very happy living over the tavern.

Pat also met some nice people who frequented the tavern. He and a woman who worked nearby as a waitress became very close, and she ended up moving in with Pat. Her name was Ellen, and she was easy-going. Like Mabel Jean, she was about 15 years older than Pat and seemed to have some of that caretaker role that Pat seemed to attract and want.

For about two months, it was a happy flat over the tavern, but then Ellen moved her daughter KC and granddaughter Katerina in with them. The granddaughter and Pat loved each other from the start, but there was some friction between KC and Pat with lots of fireworks. Then, the straw that broke the camel's back happened. Ellen also moved her son "Mutt" in "temporarily" as he searched for work after being discharged from the Army. It was chaos and Pat hated going home. He was barraged with constant pummeling with no place to go except the tavern, where he spent more and more time.

It all came crashing down when Pat put the Pepsi aside in favor of beer, got drunk, and rushed upstairs and threw Ellen and her family all out! It must have been quite a scene with lots of crying, swearing, and yelling. In the end, Pat and Dino had their happy but decrepit home back.

Another benefit of Pat hanging out in the tavern is that he met some very supportive people who remained his friends for most of his life. They were all happily married women who enjoyed spending time with Pat at the tavern and going out for lunch and dinner at their expense. Maybe this was all due to his new cool personality and emerging communication skills. Whatever it was, it worked for everyone.

Chapter 24

Pat's Unbridled Rage Destroys a Life and Our Family's Unity

Although Pat was not the same person I knew seven years ago, I still enjoyed and loved him very much. But he was now using his considerable intelligence to become somewhat cunning and vengeful. It was incomprehensible to me when I heard about the terrible deed Pat had supposedly done to one of our most beloved family members. When I confronted Pat about what I had been told, he vociferously denied having anything to do with the terrible deed. However, his defense was more than a little weak (*"How could I call the FBI; I don't even know their number"*). Anyway, he seemed sincere. I believed him and went to his defense with the family members who believed otherwise. That put Pat and I and a few other family members on one side of the biggest rift our family had ever experienced against the beloved and aggrieved victim and everyone else. The more I advocated for Pat, the worse and wider the rift became, and the less they wanted to see or hear from me.

The usually good relationships we had enjoyed in our family for so many years were no more, and it seemed nothing could heal the overt animosity on both sides. Then, there was a breakthrough that I wish had never happened: I learned that Pat had conned me. He admitted to a trusted intermediary that he vengefully and intentionally committed the terrible deed that destroyed this beloved family member's livelihood, career, and much of his and his family's lives. Once I learned that he had done this, I had to know from Pat himself if it was true. With just Pat and I present, I asked him the big question: "Did you do this?" Now comes the worst part for me of this whole awful tale. With glee and a broad smile, he answered, "Yep! I did it and I got him good, didn't I? When I went to the FBI, I sang like a canary!" I wanted to throw up! I had to get away from this awful person I thought I knew so well. I don't remember what I said when I left. Because of the subsequent pain he caused people I loved, I could not see myself ever forgiving him.

I prayed fervently for the people Pat had hurt but intentionally did not pray for Pat. After a few weeks of no contact with Pat, he called me asking for a favor. My heart and gut wanted to tell him to go to hell, but my brain brought forth the message from a recent homily regarding forgiveness (see below).

(*Romans 12:14-21*)*21 Then came Peter (what a coincidence) to him, and said, Lord, how oft shall my brother sin against me, and I forgive him? Till seven times? **22** Jesus saith unto him, I say not unto thee, Until seven times: but, Until seventy times seven.*

Seventy times seven? That is 490 times! That seemed crazy to me when the deed like Pat's was so egregious. Although I initially resisted forgiving him, this parable got to me. I must forgive him for his sake as well as mine, but a phone call changed this. Apparently, Pat was seeking forgiveness from one of the people he hurt, but they did not want to see him and asked me to keep Pat away. They were too sick medically to deal with him.

So, I did my part and told Pat to stay away from all the people he had hurt so badly. He assured me that he had no intention of approaching any of them. Okay, that task was done. Right? Wrong! Pat called this critically ill hospitalized person and begged to be allowed to come up to see them. I couldn't believe he ignored my message that came from a very ill person.

In a rage, I called him, but he said: "We worked it all out and I was forgiven." Now, I have two major things to forgive Pat for, and that equals 980 times I must forgive him. I can do it. I will do it. Maybe.

A few days after Pat's clandestine visit to the hospital, the person who forgave him died. I knew if Pat showed up at the funeral, there would possibly be a deadly confrontation. With that in mind, I begged him not to come. He said he would not, but that proved to be another lie. He did not come into the church. Instead, he sat in his beaten-up old car across the street from the church. He did the same thing at the cemetery. He told me that he waited until after everyone had left, and then he went to the grave to say goodbye. It is a deeply sad image because I know he very much loved the person who died, but I doubt that he can appreciate the awful hurt that he caused to this branch of the family.

Why did Pat commit this awful deed? Did his three burdens (high ACEs score, epilepsy, or learning disability) cause him to act in a callous and evil way? I don't think so. His lack of remorse and the glee he expressed when he said to me, "I got him good, didn't I?" is very disconcerting to me. This was not an impulsive act. It was premeditated. He planned it with delight.

Does this terrible act make Pat an evil person? I cannot think that because I do not think people are innately evil, but I do think we are all flawed. I believe Pat was perhaps more flawed than most as a result of the three major burdens he carried:

1. His high ACEs score is much attributed to the toxic stress in which we lived throughout our childhoods. His difficulties throughout his life in terms of employment and relationships could be traced back to his high ACEs score and the lack of protective factors in his life.
2. His epilepsy and the way we all coddled him made him into a demanding child and self-centered adult. He wanted things

his way but was unwilling to compromise or share what he had.

3. His learning disabilities made education beyond his ability to be successful.

It was not any single burden that caused him to take the despicable action he took that destroyed a good person, but the combination of these three burdens, coupled with a lifetime of pummelings from many sources, may have made him into a vengeful person. Just imagine the kind of person he could have been if he did not have learning disabilities, epilepsy, or the fallout from a high ACEs score. Regardless, I must forgive him and try to go forward. Harboring negative feelings and grudges is not good for anyone's mental health.

Chapter 25

Forgiveness

The residual wounds of Pat's dreadful deeds were deep and many. It was hard for me to be in his presence, and I intentionally withdrew from him. If he were to show some remorse, I may have found it easier to call him or stop by. But I could or would not, nor did he attempt to contact me. After a few weeks of indulging my angry and hurt child, I went to see him in his dismal flat over the tavern. If he was surprised and glad to see me, he didn't show either. Regardless, I forced myself to take the high road and took him to lunch. I may have done this as much for me to get away from the depressing and dirty flat where Pat chose to live.

We went to a nearby eatery where I know he likes to go. The food is good, plentiful, and cheap. The waitresses all know Pat and he plays the sad role, which elicits the patronizing responses from the waitresses that he craves. Nauseating.

Out of nowhere, a thought came to me (from above?) that I presented as a hypothetical question to Pat: "Would you ever like to live in a trailer again?"

His face lit up and he sat up. He also set the menu down. "Yeah, but I could never get one. No one rents them. You gotta buy them, and I ain't got any money."

"I might be able to help you out, but this just came to me, and I must talk to Janice, of course. Do you want to take a ride and check out some trailers after we eat?"

"Yeah, there are some out in Arcade that I looked at once with Margery. They were expensive, but they were beautiful."

"Okay. It won't hurt to look. Maybe they have some used ones. Let's eat and then do some exploring."

He was into it. He had a big toothless smile (he had all his teeth removed at the Dental School and they were going to make his dentures, but he couldn't get back there). So, now he eats a lot of soft foods and soup.

It turned out to be both a fun and productive afternoon. We drove about an hour and a half out in the country and looked at several remarkable trailers, which the salesman kept correcting us with the new name for trailers: "manufactured homes." Regardless, they were impressive but expensive. They had no used trailers (oops! manufactured homes), and so we decided to move on to other manufactured home communities closer to where I lived. When we got to the place, I wanted to checkout if we were able to look at a few used homes that might work. Pat liked them and they were in a modest but nice community. I did not say anything to Pat, but I wanted to discuss the possibility of us covering the cost of one of the homes and Pat paying the monthly lot rent, utilities, and any repairs. I told him to look over his bills and figure out what he could pay on a per-month basis. That's how we left it when I dropped him off.

After dinner, I explained to Janice (my wife) that I wanted to get Pat into a nicer place to live and my plan for how we could do it. I then got one of the biggest and best surprises of my life. She got up and went into her office and came back with a checkbook. And a mysterious smile on her face. "Here, look at this." I assumed she wanted me to look inside, and the balance was substantially more than I ever would have expected. "Where did this come from? Did you win the Lottery?"

"No, she said, it's some extra profit from my Mary Kay business that I have been putting away to surprise you with the cruise to Alaska that you always wanted us to take. I have no problem if you want to give this to Pat so he can move to a nicer place." I couldn't talk. I just hugged her for a bit before I could choke out, "Thank you. I really want us to do this for him. Let's call him right now and give this great news!" We did and, of course, blew him away.

Life is strange, especially mine. This morning, all I could think about were various ways to pummel Pat for the evil things he did to the family members that I loved and respected dearly. Now, thanks to Janice, we are buying him a MANUFAURED HOME and moving him out of the inner city and into suburbia! Very strange, indeed!

The next day, Jan and I picked up Pat and we went back out to the trailer park to pick out the best home for the best price. There were three available and we all liked one more than the other two. We learned that buying a manufactured home is a lot more like buying a car than it is like buying a regular home. We went back to the home and made sure everything worked (it did). Then, Pat's offer was accepted with just a bit of haggling, and then it was off to the office for the paperwork. Pat was a homeowner in less than two hours. We then went back to Pat's new home and did some basking while planning Pat's big move.

Because Pat always loved living in a "trailer" (that's what they called them back in 1955), his excitement was obvious. For him, it was a dream come true.

Pat gave his notice to his landlord, I rented a truck and lined up some guys to help with the move itself, and I drove Pat around to get his utilities turned on in his name. The move went smoothly, and we all pitched in to clean everything. Some neighbors stopped by to welcome Pat, and his next-door neighbor showed Pat some things he needed to know about the hot water tank.

Pat had built a substantial doghouse for Dino, but it turned out to be so solidly made that we had to leave it behind. With that, Pat announced that Dino would now be a house dog. Everybody was happy, especially Pat and Dino.

Of course, everything was not perfect. Things in the trailer broke or worked sporadically; neighbors became "difficult;" getting to the grocery and hardware stores was a problem, and coordinating his doctors' appointments (his and Dino's) were cumbersome at best. Was Pat about to be immersed in another round of pummeling with a new cast of pummelers? I hoped not.

We then made things worse for Pat when we decided to build a townhouse right behind my brother Bernie and his wife Anne Marie (Janice's sister) in the town of Victor, NY, about 90 minutes away from Pat. To lessen the burden on Pat, I arranged for Danny to provide transportation for Pat's doctors' appointments if Pat gave Danny plenty of notice.

This system collapsed almost right after it started because Danny and Pat never got along unless there was a mediator like me always present.

Despite the problems mentioned above, Pat and Dino were very happy in their new home. A bonus that we didn't appreciate was a shed that Pat quickly turned into a woodshop where he built birdhouses, various shelves for his kitchen, tool holders for inside the shed and the trailer (can't stop calling it that), and various lawn ornaments. He made friends with several neighbors who paid him to make things for them. He used this income to buy more tools and supplies, and it went on and on.

His renovations or modifications inside his trailer seemed odd to me, but they worked well for Pat. He constructed a computer workstation that housed all his music CDs, computer paraphernalia, and paperwork.

I loved stopping out to see him when I was in town (after we moved to Victor, NY). He would proudly show me his latest creations or things he was able to repair or modify. His sound system was the best, and his taste in music was outstanding. Sadly, he had to give up playing his guitar because his hands became too impaired due to carpal tunnel syndrome.

The move to Victor, NY, enabled me to come home every night from Keuka College, where I was the Chair of the Occupational Therapy Department. Prior to our moving to Victor, NY, I was gone three and sometimes four days every week. An unknown benefit of our move happened when Bernie's wife and Janice's sister Anne Marie developed cancer, requiring numerous doctors' appointments and hospital stays post-surgery, radiation therapy, and/or chemotherapy. Janice and I were able to accompany them on many of these appointments and provide the support they both desperately needed. Tragically, after a valiant fight, Anne Marie died on October 16, 2002, leaving us all devastated, especially Bernie. We also were able to support Bernie for the years following the death of Anne Marie until he met a wonderful woman only a few doors away. Janice always said that Jesus and Anne Marie teamed up to put Ann King in Bernie's life.

Once we felt Bernie was okay and our first grandchild (Luke) was born, we returned to Amherst, NY, and were only 15 minutes from Pat. I could thus resume my transportation duties and provide additional income for Pat for cutting my grass, food shopping, and other things I needed to do.

On a very sad note, Pat's beloved Dino became ill and could not be saved. After a rather brief bereavement period, Pat got a black Labrador Retriever that he named Sue after our deceased sister. Weird. This puppy was crazy right from the beginning, and Pat had very little control over her. I no longer enjoyed visiting with Pat with that crazy puppy barking, nipping, and jumping all over me as I vainly tried to relax. My visits became briefer and far less frequent.

I know Pat was lonely, but few could weather the storm of Sue the dog. It was like Sue became his current and constant pummeler, as bizarre as that sounds.

Chapter 26

Could Marriage be the Antidote for Pat's Pummeling?

Could getting married mean that my brother Pat's life of continuous pummeling would finally come to an end? I had sure hoped so at the time. I always feared that his fifty-two years of a life filled with disappointment, ridicule, failure, rejection, criticism, depression, loneliness, and other results of non-physical pummeling was going to prove too much for him to bear. I was hopeful that his neighbor, Gladys, had found the right person to be his life partner. A bonus was that she lived in the same trailer park as Pat. In fact, she was only four trailers away. Very convenient.

Historically, other women with whom Pat had had lengthy relationships were either incapable or unwilling to take on the effects of five ACEs, his limited resilience, his unresolved AD/HD, and the emotional, economic, and health issues that Pat carried. His recurring epileptic seizures that did not respond well to neurosurgery nor to a myriad of seizure-controlling drugs was a load for Pat ever since he was ten years old. Also, his increasing obesity, overeating, and sedentary lifestyle had brought his weight to over 300 pounds. We all feared he would have a stroke or a heart attack.

The list of orthopedic and neurosurgeries he experienced over the years was staggering. He willingly subjected himself to these surgeries in hopes they would result in a better life, one that would result in his being seizure-free and without pain. Sadly, these extensive surgeries did not achieve their intended objectives. So, you can add resultant anger and depression to the burdensome load of baggage he brought to any relationship. Was Gladys up to the challenges Pat brought? I was not so sure, but I remained borderline hopeful.

Let me add another item to the challenges of Pat. Now, it may seem strange to describe a 52-year-old person as spoiled, but in fact, he was. I witnessed both my mom and dad pampering Pat excessively and catering to his whims even before his epilepsy started. Of course, their indulgences were interspersed, with them both venting their frustrations with Pat's unwillingness to follow their fluctuating rules. It really annoyed the rest of us as we watched how cunning Pat could be in getting his way. Ma and Dad were saps when it came to Pat. Why? It could have been their feeling guilty for any number of reasons, like Ma having Pat later in life at age 37 or Dad's many years of carousing and drinking irresponsibly and thus leaving us in poverty. Regardless of these or other reasons, Pat was very spoiled, but don't people who are spoiled as kids become less so as they become adults? If so, Pat missed that step along the way.

However, I must recognize three strengths Pat did take with him into adulthood and into marriage. These were his mostly unrecognized keen intelligence, great sense of humor, and strong work ethic when given a job that was very hard for him to find and keep. But, despite these gifts, he still evolved into an unmotivated student, a frequently ill employee, and an impossible and selfish son, playmate, and sibling. Not surprisingly, he was unable to make friends. Cruelly, even we, his own brothers, refused to play with him. As an adult, he was always selfish, moody, ill-tempered, self-centered, demanding, and an impulsive shopper of desserts, candy, gadgets, and recorded music.

In addition to these less-than-desirable tendencies, he was in quite a bit of credit card debt. He was barely surviving on his meager Social Security Disability monthly checks that he had been receiving for the past thirty-plus years.

love each other and get along pretty good. You've also been living together for two months without any major battles. Am I right?"

They both smiled and nodded, so I decided to turn up the heat. *"So, what is stopping you from getting married?"*

Gladys broke the uneasy silence: *"We don't have the money for a nice wedding, and I don't have a dress. Also, Pat doesn't even have a sports coat."*

Time to turn up the heat a little more. *"Pat, what do you see as other things that could get in the way of you and Gladys getting married?"* I had to hear if he had some unspoken obstacle that would cause my marriage facilitation planning to blow up in my face.

"No, I would like to be married. We just can't afford it. Just like Gladys said."

Time to couple words to action and see if they are serious or just talking. *"Okay, I will pay for a small wedding (30 to 40 people), and a dress for you, Gladys and a sports coat for you, Pat. You find a church and a place where we can have a reception that I will also pay for."*

Now, to see if they were serious, I gave them some homework with a deadline. *"You two make up the guest list, pick a date, find a church you both like, get a marriage license, find a dress and sports coat, and a place for the reception. Make a list of family and friends you want to invite. When do you think you could have all this done?"*

I knew Pat could be a procrastinator, but I didn't really know Gladys. She surprised me by getting out a small notepad and making out a To-Do List. She then said, *"We should be able to get this all done in a week."*

We agreed to meet next Friday, giving them eight days to get everything done. I went home and gave the big news to my wife, Janice. She thought I was crazy. I may be, but let's see what they get done. This would be a test for Pat and Gladys. Will they pass it? I don't think so.

Chapter 27

"Going to the Chapel"

Pat and Gladys were very excited about the progress they had made. I suspected that Gladys was the one making the contacts, but if it got done, I didn't care. The church Pat frequently attended in Lockport, NY (Raymond Community Church) was able to give them a date for their wedding. It's a little church with a small congregation and is only two miles from the trailer park. Because they didn't know how much they had to spend on a reception, Gladys' wedding dress, and Pat's sports coat, they did not get anything done on these items. I gave them some parameters for the dress, sports coat, and reception and asked them to see what they could find.

When I looked at their guest list, I added some family members and friends that they hadn't thought of. We ended up with a total number of 43 people, which was just right. Gladys' daughter was taking them shopping and to a few places that might work for the reception. I couldn't believe how well this was turning out. I was feeling like some kind of wizard at wedding promotions and planning. Could this be a new career for me?

The wedding was fantastic. For starters, we were able to gather all five of the Talty brothers, and that had not happened in six years. I will never forget how good it felt to joke and kid with all of them once again. We were all very nice to Pat that day. No pummeling. We were thrilled that he was getting married, and we all thought Gladys was going to be the life partner he always wanted and needed.

It was also wonderful to see Pat in his bright green sports coat (very similar to the Masters, champion's green jacket) enjoying himself. I was impressed with how much Gladys' grandkids liked (loved?) Pat. He always loved kids and now he will be a grandpa to kids that needed him, but not nearly as much as he needed them.

Pat had made some good friends in the trailer park, and I made sure to meet all of them. They were very happy for Pat and Gladys. Those of us who knew first-hand what a hellish life Pat had been through due to the nexus of burdens he carried (5 ACEs, epilepsy, and AD/HD) seemed to be smiling more than anyone else.

For their honeymoon, they planned to enjoy the new truck Gladys had bought and just meander around New York state for a week or so. That is all the time she could get off from work. At the end of the week, they ended up at my brother Bernie and Anne Marie's house, where we were having a picnic. I was sad to see that Pat and Gladys were both in sour moods. Neither of them joined us in the usual joking and laughing that characterized our family get-togethers. They were in a funk, and I had to know why so that I could get busy fixing it.

With some gentle prodding from the annoying one (me), the cause of Pat's and Gladys' sullen moods was revealed. Gladys had a list of places in upstate New York that she always wanted to visit. Pat rejected each one and hardly talked as she drove on and on to places he refused to enter. It was evident that Gladys was both mad and confused. My brothers and I knew all too well how moody, negative, and miserable Pat can get and how stubborn he can be. Gladys was new to all this. She had to ask herself, Who is this guy I just married?

Or how do I get out of this? I prayed that they could work it out before he threw her out, which he has done to women in the past.

I had to wonder: how long can she deal with Pat's moods? Will she try to support and change him? Will he see her efforts to help as a kind of intrusion and drive him further into his negative self? Can she support and guide him into a happier and more effective adult? Could she become a much-needed protective factor in his life? I was very concerned because I pushed them both into marriage. This honeymoon was over before it even began. Will this lead to a return to Pat being pummeled? By whom? By Gladys due to her frustration? In what ways? Surprises await!

Chapter 28

Wrong Assumptions and Sad Results

I was wrong about some big things when it came to Pat and Gladys. My original premise was that a loving caregiver like Gladys would extend that love and caring to Pat. She was and is a fine person who, I think, misjudged how much she would have to give in order to make this marriage work. Those two months she lived with Pat was the only honeymoon she was going to see. His needs and wants were far greater than she knew. I think that it was during that four-day road trip that Gladys began to rethink her decision to marry Pat. However, she did not give up on the marriage. In fact, she hung in there for almost three years, which was challenging for both.

The other thing I was wrong about was my belief that Pat would or could change. He did not. He remained the rigid, spoiled person who expected everything to go his way with minimal effort on his part. I spent a lot of time with Pat as he prattled on and on about Gladys' faults. My suggestion that perhaps his stubbornness and self-centeredness perhaps was the cause of Gladys' behavior was outright rejected in angry terms. *"You're nuts, Peter and she is a bitch. I want to throw her ass out. I'm ready to go back to drinking, and it's all because of her."* Thanks to AA, he had been sober for almost twenty-five years, but he was not following the steps to remain sober. Of course, he did not want to hear this either.

Gladys and Pat attended very few family events. He would either come by himself or not at all. Also, my impromptu visits to the trailer were met with coldness from Gladys and silence from Pat. I think they were both justifiably pissed at me for railroading them into marriage, and I cannot blame them.

Gladys solved the problem by moving back into her trailer, leaving Pat back on his own. Was he depressed? Not at all. When I asked how he was handling her sudden departure, he responded in his usual way: *"I'm glad she left. I just wish she would have taken all her shit with her."* No regrets or depression on Pat's part, which I guess is good. I was the one with depression for my role in this mess.

Eventually, Gladys did come back with her son-in-law and his brother, and together, they silently moved her furnishings and clothes back to her trailer. She stayed with her daughter and grandkids for another six months and then moved out west to be near her brother. Pat's response: *"I got lots more room now and her going out West is not far enough for me."* What a guy!

Pat's bitter response to Gladys' leaving should not have surprised anyone, but it did. Especially me. So, what does the future hold for Pat? Just you wait!

Chapter 29

An Online Spark Progresses into One Hellish Infernal:

The New "Girl"

Three weeks of no calls or emails from Pat usually means things are either really good or really bad (most of the time, it's bad). I childishly tried to outlast him, but I had to know. No answer when I called and no return calls or emails. It was time for a surprise visit with Pat and his psychotic dog. Got to do it!

You always know Pat's home when you can hear his music two or three trailers away. Pounding on the door gets a response. Knocking does not.

"Hi. How come you didn't get back to me? When you don't respond, I get worried. Can you put your dog in her crate so I don't get bit and slobbered on?"

Most dogs like their crates, but not this one. She barks incessantly! Very annoying.

"I have been busy. I met a woman online from California. She's really nice. We talked for hours. Last week, we talked all night."

"All night? What about?

"Everything. She's real smart."

"Give me some details: How old? Does she work? Whereabouts in California does she live? How did you meet? When can I meet her? Let me see her picture."

"She's older, maybe 45? She doesn't have to work. She's divorced and her ex-husband is really rich, and he gives her plenty of money. He buys and sells sports memorabilia on eBay and goes to auctions and stuff. His place is in Turlock, California. I think it's near the wine country. Here's her picture."

"So, when is she coming East? Is this a current picture? She looks like the late forties or early fifties to me." Throughout these last questions and my comments, Pat is getting irritated and is shaking his head.

"She's not a morning person. She sometimes doesn't get up until 2 or 3 0'clock California time."

"What the hell. She sounds crazy. Can't wait to meet her. By the way, what's her name, and what's the name of her ex-husband's sports memorabilia company that made him so rich." Now, he's pissed!

"Look, Peter, don't go screwing this up on me. She's a good person and is nice to me. Her name is Karen Crane, and I don't know the name of his company. She might have told me. I don't know."

"I assume that talking on the phone all night and sleeping in all day doesn't leave much time to work. With her rich old man, maybe she doesn't have to work. What kind of work has she done when she did work?"

"She's got money. Don't worry about it. She had a big job at NASA. I told you she's really smart. She was way up (he gestures skyward) and in charge at Area 51 in Nevada, but it was all top-secret stuff. She can't talk about it because her job was to investigate UFOs. Like I told you, it was all top secret."

I heard enough crazy talk, and I'm sick of trying to talk over that constantly barking dog. I left wondering when Karen Crane is going to take Pat to the moon and beyond. He had a sane person in Gladys

201

as his wife, but that "didn't work out." Where are we going with Karen? Area 51? I'm worried.

All the way home, I kept wondering if Pat had stumbled into a relationship with a super con artist or with an outstanding retired NASA astronaut. I'm thinking con artist, not astronaut. Pat's warning kept popping up: "Look, Peter, don't go screwing this up on me." Sounds ominous. I wonder what he's referring to that I screwed up for him in the past.

A few weeks went by with no news about the new "girl" in Pat's life. He was excited when we finally talked. "Karen's coming to stay with me for a couple of weeks."

"Let me get this straight. Is she leaving someplace in sunny California to come to snowy Lockport, New York, in January? Didn't you say that she was real smart?"

"She is smart. She just likes cooler weather. Her husband pays for everything, even a rental car, the whole time she is here. I have got to get busy and get this place cleaned up. It's kind of messy because of Sue (his dog)."

I was sure concerned to hear how this Karen Crane thing is getting more and more bizarre. Who is she really? What does she want from Pat? I have mixed feelings. I fear for Pat. Is she going to turn out to be the master pummeler in his life, or has Pat just won the lottery with a rich "girl" who can solve all his financial problems?

I told him, "Let me know when she arrives so I can make a trip to Lockport to meet this rich and brilliant "girl." I was oozing sarcasm, which made Pat angry. "I don't care what you say. She's good to me."

"Let me know as soon as she gets to Lockport. I'll wait by the phone (more sarcasm. I can't stop!")

"Screw you!"

That's clear!

Chapter 30

She's Here!

Of course, the "she" is in reference to Karen Crane, who recently arrived from California. The only reason I know this is because he sent me the message above but no other information. I called him after 10:00 pm and had this meaningless conversation:

"So, when did Karen get to your place."

"I don't know. When did you get here?" to Karen, who takes the phone from Pat and takes off on a travel monologue: "I came as fast as I could because I missed my man. Enterprise is the best! The kid brought me right to my man's door, and then he took the car back to the airport or some other designated place but easily accessible Enterprise lot. Why is the car sitting here and costing me money if we don't need it? If we are going to venture out from our cozy den, I will just call Enterprise, and they will bring a car to us. I will drop the driver back at their lot, or they may send a second car. So, it's all set. Don't you worry about it? Good night, Peter." With that, she hung up. I have not yet met this woman, but I do not like her dismissive and take-charge attitude.

Three days later, I had the time off, so I made a surprise visit to the so-called "Cozy Den." There was no one answering the door, but I could hear muffled talking in conjunction with a lot of barking. I decided to wait a bit and then knock some more. I repeated this a few more times and then changed my approach: "Hey Karen. It's Pat's brother Peter who made the two-hour drive over treacherous, snow-covered roads just to meet you. Pat explained to me that you're not a morning person, but I figured it being 3:30 in the afternoon would be a good time to meet and take you two out to dinner. How does that sound?" More muffling and, of course, continuous barking.

Pat came to the door but didn't open it. In a low volume, he simply said, "This is not a good time."

"Do you think you could be ready to go in an hour? I'll come back."

More mumbling. "No, it's not a good day at all."

"Okay. What would be a good day? I have flexibility in my schedule and can come back any day you pick. What would be best?"

"Any day next week after 3:00 o'clock, but call first." (this was the bitch's voice calling the shots).

I drove home for two hours in my enraged state and was unpleasant to an undeserving Janice all evening. This was not to say I didn't think about the two of them in the "Cozy Den" up in Lockport. I think this may be one of those situations in which I detest responsibility over which I have no control. Very aggravating!

Chapter 31

Merry Christmas!

A month went by without contact with Pat. No phone calls, emails, telegrams, knocks on my door, or smoke signals from Pat (nor Karen). However, apparently, we will be getting together on Christmas Eve! I, too, was surprised! My son Peter and his wife Kathy are hosting a little family get-together at their home, and there will be two *special guests* (italics are mine): Luke, our new grandson's first Christmas and Karen, Pat's *special California friend* (again, italics mine). I don't know how it happened, but Peter invited Pat and Karen was included. Lucky me!

Also, it was a great night for Pat because he was able to give us all our Christmas gifts. Due to his financial struggles over the past twenty years, this was something he has been unable to do. He was very proud to pass out the gifts, and I was happy for him.

At least tonight, I get to meet Karen and perhaps get some of my many questions asked and answered before one of us pouts and leaves the party early. I think it's 50/50 who bails first, Karen or me? Probably me. Ugh!

She was not what I expected. Karen was initially quite friendly and responded to my questions easily but exhaustingly. When it comes to making conversation, I would describe Karen as monopolistic. I remember noticing that she was not curious about Janice, me, or anyone else at the little gathering. What was troubling to me was that Pat was very lethargic and after distributing his gifts, he slept almost the whole night away. I kept waking him up and tried to get him to engage in a conversation but was unsuccessful.

I wondered, was it drugs that made Pat so lethargic? Was it some concoction she put together drawing on her great intelligence that Pat was always raving about?

If a measure of intelligence was the ability to talk, then Karen was another Einstein. She talked nonstop for almost fifteen long, boring minutes (I was covertly timing her) in response to this question: "Pat told me that your former husband has a very successful sports memorabilia business. How did he get into that?" I think she went back to her former husband's Kindergarten experience in 'Duck, Duck, Goose,' but she never got him out of high school (joke). It was maddening. I couldn't get a word in or ask for clarification. I then did a very rude thing that I still feel very good about today. Without a word to Karen, I got up in the middle of one of her many run-on sentences, walked across the room, and talked with my son-in-law Dan with my back to Karen. Ill-mannered? Oh yes, but the child in me was delighted.

There was one exchange between Pat and Karen that also troubled me. Because Karen, Pat, and I were next to each other on the couch, I could overhear their conversations as minimal as they were:

Pat wakes up, looks around quizzically like he doesn't immediately recognize us or where he is, but says nothing.

Karen looks mildly concerned with a sickeningly sweet smile and asks Pat in a patronizing, motherly voice: "How do you feel?"

Pat mutters weakly: "Tense."

"Do you want to go?" Pat nods feebly. Then, without a word of thanks to our host and hostess or a word to the rest of us, she asked my son for their coats. Peter (my son) helps Pat get his coat on with the help of Karen. She then puts hers on quickly. Pat waves weakly to us all, and out they go. All very strange.

I, of course, have many more questions without answers: Was Pat drugged? Did Karen put a spell on him? Am I being overly concerned about Pat? Why does she talk so much? What's wrong with her?

Chapter 32

What Have I Learned about Karen?

After a one-month stay, Karen went back to California. She told Pat that she loved the Western New York winters and couldn't wait to come back. Pat was looking forward to her return. I was not, but I didn't have to live with her or listen to her wild tales of success and achievement that go on and on (without a comma). It was also good that Karen was back in California because this meant I could visit Pat again and just try to cope with his hyper-out-of-control dog, Sue. However, after only a month or so of tranquility, "the hurricane" was back, and I was no longer allowed to visit.

Now, one thing I know about Pat is that he minimizes, exaggerates, or outright lies about events in his life. To confuse any fact-finding effort even further, he is usually telling the truth. Ever since Karen has returned, I have been trying to establish which of the following statements of Pat's about Karen are true: I will attach an asterisk next to each one that I know or believe to be true:

- She is a germaphobe*.
- She is rich.
- She is a shopaholic*.
- She hits and threatens to hit Pat constantly.
- Every time Pat comes in from outside, Karen makes him strip in the enclosed porch and then shower. *
- She will not let any mail come into the house until it has sat on the enclosed porch for 24 hours to be sure all germs are eradicated. *
- She is divorced.

- She is crazy and throws raging tantrums anytime her many rules are not followed. *
- No one is allowed in the trailer except Pat.*
- He cannot make any phone calls without her listening to every word, and she reads all his emails (incoming and outgoing) *

As a summary, I would say that if all the above are true, then Pat was "under siege," and the English Dictionary provides a very apropos definition of this state: *If someone or something is under siege, they are being severely criticized or put under a great deal of pressure.* It sure sounds a lot like pummeling to me.

He told me about these things on his cell phone while walking his dog. In responding to Pat's phone messages, I had to be very discreet and even more so in emails because she was always checking his communication. Here is one I remember sending him when he first informed me about what was going on:

"Hey Pat, I was just thinking about all the trash you have all over your place left over from your renovation projects. Just say the word and I'll come out there and haul all that crap away for you... How about tomorrow afternoon? You can pick the time. No one should have to live with all that trash." (by "trash," I, of course, meant Karen).

It is obvious from Pat's response below that my cleverly disguised message was not understood.

"What trash are you talking about? I got rid of all my scrap wood and garbage right after I finished renovating the kitchen and living room. I don't have any trash around. What are you talking about?"

Because I tended to believe Pat, and her leaving sunny California and coming to upstate New York in mid-winter indicates that she doesn't have the best judgment, all indicated to me that Pat needed help. I don't know why he was so afraid of her. He outweighed her by 75 pounds. Also, in my clinical experience, I do not think she is psychotic, but there is a diagnostic condition that fits her quite well: Borderline Personality Disorder. According to the DSM-V, in general, *"individuals with personality disorders may have no insight into the role that their own behavior plays in creating problems within their environment. They may rationalize their actions, blaming others for their situation or misfortune without examining their own responsibility for the situation at hand."*

Below are more details from the DSM-5 on Borderline Personality Disorder that include some epidemiology and demographics, and more importantly, the signs and symptoms that are used to make this diagnosis. Based on my clinical experience with people diagnosed with borderline personality disorder, my interactions with and observations of Karen, photographs Pat sent me of the inside of Karen's California home, the excessive cleaning supplies that Karen bought and left behind that I observed in Pat's trailer, and Pat's descriptions of Karen's bizarre behavior I see Karen having most of the characteristics of this disorder. In this vein, below, I placed an asterisk after each and every sign or symptom that is consistent with Karen's personality and behavior.

Borderline Personality Disorder Definition:

Borderline personality disorder is defined as a mental illness that significantly impacts a person's emotional regulation, according to the National Institute of Mental Health (NIMH).[1] This dysregulation can result in increased impulsivity*, poor self-esteem*, and difficulty in relationships with others*.[2] People with the disorder are often uncertain about their identity, often causing rapid shifts in their interests*, and they tend to view situations and other people in terms of extremes, such as all good or all bad*.[2]

Usually diagnosed in late adolescence or early adulthood, borderline personality disorder (BPD) affects 5.9% of US adults at some time in their lives, representing about 14 million Americans and accounting for 20% of patients admitted to psychiatric hospitals and 10% of people in outpatient mental health treatment. Of those with BPD, women account for 70% of patients. [1-4]

CRITERIA

DSM-5 Diagnostic Criteria for BPD

The term "borderline" was first used to denote the condition's position between psychosis and neurosis. [4] Although the word does not describe the disorder well, the term has remained. [4]

In the fifth edition of the Diagnostic and Statistical Manual of Mental Disorders (DSM-5), the criteria for borderline personality disorder considered a personality disorder, are defined as a pervasive pattern of instability in interpersonal relationships*, self-image*, and affects*, and marked impulsivity* beginning by early adulthood and present in a variety of contexts, * as indicated by five or more of the following:

- Fear of abandonment*

- Unstable or changing relationships*.

- Unstable self-image, including struggles with a sense of self and identity*.

- Stress-related paranoia*

- Anger regulation problems, including frequent loss of temper or physical fights*.

- Consistent and constant feelings of sadness or worthlessness*

- Self-injury, suicidal ideation, or suicidal behavior

- Frequent mood swings*

- Impulsive behaviors such as unsafe sex, reckless driving, binge eating*, substance abuse, or excessive spending. *

Many of these behaviors were not evident when Karen was visiting Pat but spewed forth throughout the time he lived with Karen and her husband in California.

Chapter 33

Karen's Surprises Pat and Her Invitation is Readily Accepted

Big news: Karen has a husband; they are not divorced, and he is on his way to Lockport to stay in the one-bedroom trailer with Pat, Karen, and the insane dog Sue. How is that for three big surprises? Also, there were even more surprises (see below). When I asked Pat some basic questions, like why is he coming? How long is he staying? Why did Karen keep up the lie about them being divorced? Who is not going to get a bed (Pat only has one double bed and a loveseat)? Will Karen's husband have to follow the same rules as stripping and showering every time he comes into the trailer from outside?

Not surprising Pat did not know the answers to my questions, and not surprising he was not curious or brave enough to ask the "BIG Cheese" Karen for the answers. I cannot wait to see how all this turns out.

I heard nothing from Pat for almost two weeks. I sent him innocuous emails and left phone messages composed so they would not arouse Karen's ire. When I finally did get a response, he was very excited because they (Karen, her husband Travis, and Pat) were out shopping. Pat said, "It's like the Christmases rich kids have on TV. They buy me anything I want, and they buy anything they want. Travis is a good guy, and he must be rich in the way they spend money and fill up the little car he rented. I got to go. Travis wants to show me something."

All that talk about Travis being rich was a lie. According to Pat, Travis was not rich, and although he bought and sold a few pieces of sports memorabilia, he did not own a business of any sort. However, he was a supervisor at a large factory. The spending spree they were presently on was supported by the remortgaging of their house, something they had done twice before.

Besides having two shopaholics living in his trailer, Pat had a crisis involving his seizure medication. About three years ago, Pat's doctor had prescribed two new medications that had produced miraculous results. He was seizure-free for over two years, and Dr. Zoll signed the form authorizing Pat to drive. He was able to buy a cheap used car and loved the freedom this brought him. He and his dog loved the open road!

However, something changed, and Pat started having mild seizures again. After an exhaustive search, Dr. Zoll could not find a medication or dosage that would work as well as the previous ones. So, Pat did not want to hurt anybody, so he surrendered his driver's license and sadly sold his cherished car. But Dr. Zoll continued to search for an effective medication, and again, he was successful, but with a drawback: the new medication was very expensive (about ($1,100 per month), and it was not covered under New York's Medicaid program. Neither I nor my siblings were able to cover this, so Pat was on his own. I always saw this as a bureaucratic form of pummeling.

I do not know how it came about, but Pat decided to sell his trailer and go live with Karen and Travis in California. I think it was Horace Greeley who famously said, "Go west, you jerk, go west!" I'm paraphrasing, of course, and just reacting to this, the greatest shock of all.

Pat was very excited and refused to reconsider this bold and questionable move with Karen as the wagon master. I believe the biggest reason to move to California is that Pat discovered that his seizure medication would be covered under their Medicaid program known as Medi-Cal. This would save him over $13,000 per year, plus Karen and Travis said that he could live rent-free in their house.

It seemed like this was a great opportunity for Pat, but I had my concerns about him living with someone with Karen's obvious psychological dysfunctions indicative of a person with the potential diagnosis of borderline personality disorder. I was glad to hear that Pat was going to ride out there with Karen and Travis and assess the whole situation before he made the decision to make California his new home or not.

Travis took the small car back to Enterprise and got an SUV that could accommodate the three of them, their luggage, lots of snacks, and Wild Dog. When they asked Pat what he would like to see traveling west, his only request was that he get to see the town of Talty, Texas. After a few more days, they were off with Travis doing all the driving. To add to the excitement of Pat's first cross-country trip, Karen declared that she would buy Pat a T-shirt and an ice cream sundae in every state they traveled through.

Pat sent me a photo on his phone of himself smiling, standing next to a Talty, Texas sign. He also collected his T-shirts and ice cream sundaes in every state as promised. There was, however, a bit of a disappointment for Pat when they were traveling through New Mexico. It was Pat's intention to stop to visit our oldest brother, Tommy, and his wife, Karoline, who lived just outside of Albuquerque. However, Tommy did not think it was a good idea because he did not know the people Pat was traveling with, and his wife Karoline was very ill. Pat was disappointed but accepted Tommy's decision, and they continued their way to California.

Overall, it was a good trip. Apparently, they laughed a lot, and there were no fights or tantrums along the way. Pat loved the California weather. Having lived almost his whole life where cold and lake effect snowstorms were a way of life, the California sun was wonderful. After about six weeks of the California lifestyle, he was just about sold on moving out there. The clincher was that by using Karen's address, he could qualify for Medi-Cal and not have to pay for his high-priced seizure medication. He returned to his trailer in Lockport with a single-minded focus: sell everything and permanently relocate to California. I hated to see him leave, but I understood what motivated him to do it.

Chapter 34

California Dreaming

Pat was difficult to be around once he wanted to be in California with Karen, Travis, and Wild Dog. He was not interested in the family and what was going on in our lives. His heart and mind had gone west, and nothing back east was of interest to him. Karen did a great job of brainwashing him. We were out and Karen and Travis were in.

In helping him clean out his trailer and beloved workshop, I was amazed at how little he cared about the things he once treasured. He had a lot of nice tools, and I thought we could clean them up, put a fair price on each one and run a yard sale that also included his household goods. He rejected all of that because Karen told him to just give the stuff away because they were going to buy all new stuff for him. She showed him an area in the garage that would be his work area with new tools she would buy him. The same thing happened with his household goods. Oh, well, it's his stuff.

The sale of his trailer had not gone well. Only a few potential buyers went through it, but they didn't come back or make even a lowball offer. Janice and I prepared and sold five of our homes without a realtor, so I told Pat some things that I thought might be turning potential buyers away. First, the house was filthy and cluttered. Before Karen returned to California, she stockpiled extensive amounts of cleaning supplies, paper towels, toilet paper, Lysol, and so forth. All closets and cabinets were full to bulging, and every horizontal surface had an assortment of food scraps on plates and bowls and empty pizza boxes wedged in between. This collection of garbage, combined with the strong scent of Wild Dog, would turn any potential buyer away. None of this was of concern to Pat. Frustrating!

I say Pat's demeanor was one of irritation and I know I was the unintentional irritator. I keep recalling the old images of Pat being so proud of his trailer and always trying to improve it. Those days are gone and never to return. The message to self is just get over it! If he doesn't care, then why should I? With that new perspective, I joined Pat's program of: "I don't care; he's out of here." So, in the most passive-aggressive way, I used the magic marker and began making signs that I began taping on many, many items that said: "FREE! HELP YOURSELF! BRAND NEW! NEVER BEEN OPENED, OWNER OUT OF HERE ASAP. EVERYTHING MUST GO, OPEN TO OFFERS ON TRAILER, TELL YOUR FRIENDS, etc. Pat was laughing and liked my crazy approach.

Regardless, word spread around the trailer park and shelves and cupboards were emptying fast. However, when it came to Pat's tools, stereo equipment, his computer, and electronics stuff, he took my signs off that stuff. He said, "I have to think about these things." Okay, at least we're getting the place de-cluttered, and maybe a good cleaning can happen next. I'm ready to clean, but Pat says, "That's enough for today."

In some ways, I accomplished more than I initially thought I could. Now, I can say that Karen is a shopaholic, a germaphobe, and a hoarder driven by OCD. I shared this with Pat, but he defended Karen. "I don't care about all that. She is good to me." He said this so vehemently that I knew there was no use pointing out how he was getting himself into a very challenging living situation, and there was no turning back.

Since my frustration meter was on DANGER, I was fine with quitting for the day. When I asked if he wanted me to come back tomorrow, he paused and said, "Yes, but don't come before 11:00

o'clock and don't be so bossy." My childish side was ignited, and I said, "Let's leave it at this: I won't come back until you call me. You good with that?"

"Yeah, but don't wait by the phone. Don't call me; I'll call you."

With that childish exchange, I left, but of course, I caved. I called him the next morning and took him out for breakfast at his favorite restaurant, where most of the waitresses knew him by name. Neither of us brought up California, Karen, or the trailer. He did bring up that a young woman in the trailer park might take over his lease and Pat would just give her the trailer as is. When he ran down the things that needed to be repaired or replaced, Pat may be getting the better part of the deal. The real bonus is that she told Pat that he didn't have to clean it. She'll do it because she likes to clean. Looks like we can cross trailer-cleaning off my worry list! Done!

Pat had boxed up a bunch of stuff and I took him to the post office. I think he had nine boxes that he shipped west.

All my life, I have dreaded endings. They make me very depressed and Pat going to California forever made me very sad. Of course, I couldn't say this to him because he is as excited about moving to California as he was back in 1954 when he, Ma, and Danny took the train to Texas. Back then, he was glad, and I was sad, just like now.

I didn't get to see him again before he left, but his plan was to come back and finalize the transfer of the trailer and a few other things.

When he returned, he was all excited about the three Lazy Boy lounge chairs Karen bought for each of them and a motorized scooter she bought Pat. With this, he could get to church, go for coffee, and explore the community. He loved the freedom it gave him.

The transfer of the trailer went smoothly, and Pat felt good that he could give his trailer to a young woman who would probably never be able to buy one. Pat's next-door neighbor, who is very handy, volunteered to do a lot of the fixing that needed to be done. I think Pat felt like the white knight who rode in and rescued the damsel in distress or something like that.

Pat was flying out the next morning, so I took him out for lunch. We had a good time. I dropped him off, hugged him goodbye, and drove home crying like I am doing now as I type this.

Chapter 35

Pummeler Extraordinaire!

None of us was prepared for the extent and nature of the pummelings Pat experienced once he was settled in California. I knew Karen had problems with interpersonal relationships, which is the hallmark of borderline personality disorder (BPD), but the extent to which she became unhinged with histrionics is unfathomable. "Histrionics" are exaggerated dramatic behaviors designed to attract attention, and "unfathomable" is not too strong a word to describe Karen being out of control in the numerous situations that Pat relayed to me using his cell phone while he tooled about the community on his scooter.

It may be helpful to re-visit the signs and symptoms of BPD with the asterisks next to the ones Karen clearly demonstrates:

Remember, BPD is a pervasive pattern of instability in interpersonal relationships*, self-image and affects*, and marked impulsivity beginning by early adulthood and present in a variety of contexts, * as indicated by five or more of the following: [5]

- Fear of abandonment*

- Unstable or changing relationships*.

- Unstable self-image, including struggles with a sense of self and identity*.

- Stress-related paranoia*

- Anger regulation problems, including frequent loss of temper or physical fights*.

- Consistent and constant feelings of sadness or worthlessness*

- Self-injury, suicidal ideation, or suicidal behavior

- Frequent mood swings*

- Impulsive behaviors such as unsafe sex, reckless driving, binge eating*, substance abuse, or excessive spending. *

Pat described dozens of incidents that are emblematic of a person with BPD where Karen demonstrates all these elements: she goes off without provocation, reacts in an emotionally exaggerated way, blames someone else, and has zero insight into her role in the mess that resulted.

As you read this vignette, think about the elements of BPD listed above. Here is the incident that I feel shows Karen demonstrating many of the elements of BPD: Pat, Karen, and Travis were on their way to what I think Pat said was a family reunion. I do not know whose family, but it doesn't really matter. As usual, Travis was driving and suddenly Karen began screaming at Travis and then she began to punch him repeatedly as he tried to keep control of the car. It became too much for Travis, who at this point was crying, and he pulled the car over onto the shoulder, got out, and began walking away. Pat also got out of the car, caught up with Travis, put his arm around him, and brought the distraught man back to the car. By this time, Karen had the back gate of the SUV open and was screaming obscenities as she scraped the food from two large pans of casseroles she had prepared for the reunion into the bushes. With that, she then threw the empty pans into the back, got in the car, and announced to Travis: "We're going back home. You ruined a nice day, and I'm going to tell them that we couldn't come because of you."

To appreciate what Pat is experiencing on an ongoing basis, I mentioned earlier that Pat sent me photographs of each room of

Karen and Travis' house, including the garage. The amount of clutter is reminiscent of the worst homes of the people you see on TV if you watch the show, *Hoarders.* Each room shows an amazing amount of stuff. Pat said he just stays in his room or goes out on his scooter.

It is probably best that Pat gets out of the way of the fray that is sure to come from Karen with little to no provocation. Remember, one of the key characteristics of BPD is *anger regulation problems, including frequent loss of temper or physical fights.* Once these eruptions occur, there is no reasoning with Karen, and Pat knows this, but Travis apparently does not. He courageously tries to reason with Karen or tries to placate her, all to no avail. Walking on eggshells, pins, and needles, between a rock and a hard place, and many other platitudes are all apt descriptions of the erupting maelstrom for those around Karen.

Pat kept and shipped his treasured items like his complete set of videotapes of The Honeymooners, Green Acres, and other selected TV shows he loved. This was his escape. As Pat saw the telltale signs of one of Karen's meltdowns about to commence, he slipped into his bedroom, popped in a favorite video, put his earphones in, and relaxed. His scooter provided the same kind of escapism. The only time these avoidance behaviors didn't work was when her rage was focused on Pat. His efforts to use his interpersonal skills to help resolve a problem that she said he had created were totally inadequate. No, this was when Karen's vast skills of manipulation intertwined with bombastic speech went on and on until she exhausted herself. She proved to be an outstanding pummeler, and Pat and Travis were no match for her.

In our phone conversations, he and I would get to laughing over how crazy she was. Her behavior and the way she attacked Travis and Pat were completely devoid of logic. I was able to provide Pat with validation that the things she brought up to pummel him with were her own creation and, thus were not valid. She was so clever and diabolical that she could get people like Pat and Travis to feel they were at fault. It was never Karen's.

I don't know what triggered it, but on one phone call, he sounded so helpless and hopeless. It may have been that his back was bothering him to the extent that he couldn't ride his scooter. He was stuck in the house and thus was an easy target. The conversation started off with his telling me: "I screwed up big time coming out here. I paid for everything to get us out here: the gas, the car rental, five nights in motels, and all the food we ate. When I told Karen and Travis that I had a big bill on my credit card, she gave me $50.00."

I interrupted him to ask: "What happened to all the money you said they had?"

"That was another bunch of lies. You should see their house. It needs a lot of work; I think they re-mortgaged it three times."

"Can't you move out?"

"I could, but when I ask them to take me down to the Welfare office, Karen goes crazy crying and begging me not to leave and she also promises to change. I feel sorry for her and tell her I'll stay. I thought of coming back home, but I have no place to stay, and I would have to come up with the $1,100 per month for my seizure medicine that New York state doesn't cover. I'm screwed!"

Yes, he was screwed. He was stuck in a terrible living situation with no other options. Of course, he was screwed, but we were pissed. We knew the situation and were concerned, but he had that "Talty one-track mind" and could see nothing but the picture of Shangri-La that Karen had painted in his mind. It was as if once he got to California, all would be fine. Oh, yeah, and those little behavioral miscues of Karen's were no big deal and would surely disappear once she got home. What a bunch of hogwash she sold to Pat and put him in a classic no-win situation.

No one in the family, either individually or collectively, has the resources to relocate Pat back to Western New York, give him the down payment on a decent trailer, and also give him the $1,100 per month to cover his seizure medication. So, in effect, we were all screwed along with Pat.

I had no words of encouragement for Pat. I was initially too mad and too sad, but within the same conversation, I drew on my clinical and personal experience with alcoholism as expressed by AA. Knowing that Pat was a member of the AA fellowship, I knew he would see the value of my suggestion to get to a meeting and talk this out. My other suggestion also came from AA but is also consistent with our Catholic faith: turn it over to a higher power by going to church. He liked both ideas, but let's see what he does with them.

Chapter 36

Pummeling Shifts from Mental to Physical

(Medical)

I did not receive any phone calls from Pat for about two weeks, and I was hoping that he had found my suggestions so helpful that he had immersed himself in AA and his church. WRONG! I hardly recognized his voice when he finally picked up. He was in great pain in his back along the left side. It seemed Karen thought all he needed was her special massages, rest, and some relaxation exercises that she taught him. After a week, they decided to take Pat to the hospital. In the Emergency Room, he was diagnosed with the Flu, and they sent him home.

After only a few days, his pain was so bad that Karen and Travis took Pat back to the hospital, where he was admitted.

I was concerned that Pat may not have his facts straight, and so I got Karen's cell phone number after I finished talking with Pat. It was a short conversation because of his pain.

However, it was not a short conversation with Karen. It never is because of her high need to control everything, especially conversations. It took me twenty minutes to get the main reason for my call: the name and contact number of Pat's doctor. But she also gave me the worst news ever about Pat: he was diagnosed with untreatable pancreatic cancer. It was an awful shock to the extent that my crying forced me to hang up on her. I told Janice and we cried together. I also said, "If there is nothing they can do for him, I would like to fly out to California, rent an SUV, and drive him and his dog back here to our house to be around family for whatever time he had. What do you think?" Her response was classic Janice: "I think we should do it. Do you want me to go with you?" Because it is important that we have the house ready, I was conflicted about her offer. Having been an OT doing home care with people who were terminally ill, I knew there was a lot to be done and responded with my brain and not my broken heart: "I would love you along the whole way, but I need you to get things ready back here. If all goes well, I would like to fly out two days from now and be back here with him and his dog five or six days later. It all depends on how impaired Pat is. Some of the things you can do are get him on Hospice, order a hospital bed and a commode, and have Grab Bars installed next to the toilet and in the shower. I'll type out a list for you. Of course, none of this will be needed if he is too ill to travel or if he prefers to die in California. It's his call."

I called Karen back, apologized, and then said I had to call Pat. She understood. I intentionally did not tell her about Janice's and my plan to bring him back here. I wouldn't want her to misinterpret our intentions.

Pat was more stoic about the news than I. His calm demeanor helped me to stay in control. I then told him what Janice and I wanted to do and that the plan included his dog. I did not need to mention that he would be leaving a crazy house and coming to a calm house where friends and relatives could come to visit.

His response was sad in some ways: "You guys would do all this for me?"

"Absolutely. We love you and it would be an honor to help you in any way we can. I must call your doctor to hear what he thinks about you making the trip. I'll let you know what he says. Also, don't say anything to Karen and Travis. Let me explain it."

He was very happy and even joked: "If my doctor doesn't okay the trip, I'll just fire his ass."

His doctor was very nice. After I explained what we wanted to do, he said: "I think it is an excellent idea for Pat to be back home and to be around loved ones. There is nothing we can really do for him here except provide comfort care. However, the sooner he makes the trip, the better. He does not have much time left." Wow! That whacked me then, as it still does over 15 years later. I thanked him but had to hang up quickly to regain control so I could coherently make some difficult phone calls.

I first called Janice and told her Pat was very appreciative of our plan. I next called Bernie, the first of my brothers I wanted to call. Bernie was shocked, but he quickly shifted into his usual helpful mode and said, "I'll come with you. I'll get Janice and Ann (my sister-in-law) working on flights out of Buffalo ASAP. We can split the driving and make the trip as pleasant as we can for him. I still can't believe it."

The inability to grasp that Pat was dying was something both Danny and Tommy expressed. I was not surprised at their response because I felt the same thing, and this demonstrates how close we still are after all these years. It is a beautiful thing. My being the only one now left of six makes me miss them all every day.

Chapter 37

The Trip to Bring Pat Home

Janice and Ann did some fine coordination and got us flights out of Buffalo and into the closest California airport, which put us two and a half hours from Pat's hospital. They also arranged for us to rent a Ford Expedition large enough to enable us to put Wild Dog in a large crate that Travis would get for us. I had talked with Pat the night before and told him that Bernie was also coming, which made him very happy. However, when we were in line in Chicago getting ready to board the flight to California, my cell phone rang, and it was Pat. He was in a very agitated state. I made what I thought was a funny comment, but he lashed out, "Peter, this is no joke! You gotta get here fast." I was next in line to board, so I only had time to say, "We are getting on the plane right now. We will see you in a few hours. We love you." That was the last time I talked to Pat.

The rest of the flight was uneventful, but the car rental place was not. It was a smaller airport, and we were the only customers at the car rental desk. They had our reservation but not our Expedition! They tried to talk us into taking a smaller SUV like a Chevy Blazer, but after about an hour of waiting impatiently, they said our vehicle had arrived. Because they could not come up with a Ford Expedition, they gave us a Cadillac Escalade instead. We were pleased. Very pleased! We also agreed that Pat would love it.

We had directions to the hospital and so went directly there. It was dark by this time, and we had trouble seeing where to park and where the entrance was. We inadvertently walked in through the Emergency Room, which had a waiting room filled with a lot of crying kids and exhausted parents. The Security Guard sent us down a hall, took the elevator to the third floor and went looking for Pat. He was not easy to find. We mistakenly woke a man who we were certain was Pat. A check of his wristband made our mistake evident. The Security Guard must have given us the wrong floor or room number, and this turned out to be the case. A kindly nurse appeared and took us to his room, offered her condolences, and explained that he had been agitated earlier tonight (talking to me on the phone?) but resting comfortably now. She suggested that we try waking him because he has not been responding to them for the last few hours. We went in, but it didn't look like Pat, so I checked his wristband, and it was him. We called his name several times and shook him a little more than gently and there was no response. He was breathing softly, and he did not seem to be in any pain or distress.

While we were with Pat, Karen, and Travis came in, and Pat's lack of response greatly alarmed her. She went to talk to the nurse. Why didn't we think of that? When Karen came back in, she had the nurse with her. Karen had her take-charge-confrontational hat on and was rather rude as she tried to find out what happened to Pat. The nurse was great in the way she was professional but held her own when she stated: "Well, you realize he is dying, and he is entering one of the final stages of this process." She then turned to Bernie and me and said, "You must be his brothers from out of town. It's so nice you came. I'm Nancy Comstock." Wow, she really made Karen look like the jerk she was!

Bernie and I, along with Travis and Karen, took turns sitting with Pat so that if he did wake up, he wouldn't be alone. Karen and Travis left for dinner for an hour or so, and while they were gone, our brother Pat died without ever waking up. No more pummeling Pat. Rest in the peace you so deserved. Love you.

We called Ann and Janice to give them the news as we did with Karen and Travis upon their return. We then got down to business, and I explained what Pat wanted to be done. He wants to be cremated and buried with our Dad in Hillcrest Cemetery in Armor, New York. He liked the idea of a family picnic in his favorite park, Chestnut Ridge, as a celebration of his life. He hoped Karen and Travis would keep his dog and they would like that. Travis said, "I'm glad I kept the receipt for the crate I bought. I can get my money back. Nancy, the nurse, stopped by to give us some contact information on some local funeral homes for us to call. The nurses would prepare Pat's body for transfer and would have him ready whenever the funeral director wanted to pick him up.

It was a long, sad, and exhausting day for us all. Bernie and I went out for a late spaghetti dinner, where we got the only laugh of the day when he saw the largest meatball we had ever seen on a side plate that Bernie had ordered. We slept well and had breakfast before going over to the Funeral home we had called and planned for him to be cremated and his ashes mailed to my house.

Then it was back to the airport and on our way back home. One hell of a trip. On our way to the airport, we called Tommy and Danny and filled them in on all that had taken place and the arrangements for Pat's burial. We were done in more ways than one.

Chapter 38

The Threats and Pummelings of Karen are No More!

If I did not view Karen through the lens of my knowledge of mental illness, especially Borderline Personality Disorders (BPD), I would be very frustrated and confused about her behavior and motivation. I so much appreciated Pat providing me with his detailed observations of a few of the hundreds of Karen's meltdowns, bizarre habits, and distorted views of everything. I did not put this all together until after Pat's passing. This eureka experience or epiphany came to me after Janice and I spent three and a half hours listening to Karen talking nonstop and not touching her dinner, but I must explain.

Once I was back home, I had many exchanges of emails and phone conversations with Karen, all centered on one thing: the contents of Pat's bedroom. I knew it contained many things that would have emotional memories for members of our family. However, Karen kept telling me that she still, after six weeks, was unable to enter his bedroom. I think I caught her at a weak moment, and she agreed that Janice and I could come to California a week after this phone conversation took place in order to go through Pat's room. Janice immediately booked flights for both of us, rented a car, made hotel reservations for three nights, and notified Karen of our plans. I insisted on meeting them for dinner with us at an Applebee's near their home and our hotel. She agreed that the dates would be fine.

Janice and I waited 45 minutes for them to arrive and when they finally did, there was no apology nor explanation for making us wait. Not a good start.

Her constant talking required no response from her audience. I tried to segue into when we could come to the house at least a dozen times without success. Her monologue reminded me of a line from the late and great George Carlin, who said of a girl's speech he knew that "she carried on without a comma." That was Karen. She didn't eat and took her whole dinner home.

After three and a half hours of her meandering yapping, I had had enough and cut her off with a firm voice up a notch in volume and purposely stated why we came: "Okay Karen, we have had a long day and need to know what time tomorrow we can go through Pat's bedroom."

"Oh, tomorrow won't work. I must go to my mother's."

Travis speaks: "I can meet them and let them in." Yeah, Travis!

"NO, NO, NO. You must go with me. I need you over there." Travis did not speak again.

Karen was back in charge: "Call me tomorrow and I will see what I can work out."

Then began three fruitless days of many phone calls, text messages, and unanswered emails, along with numerous trips to their house at all hours with no one answering the door. On our final day, when we were at the airport, Karen called with another monologue that I cut off with something about the economic and emotional of this wasted trip.

What could be her motivation for her diabolical manipulations to prevent us from searching Pat's bedroom? As an explanation, I return to the list of signs and symptoms she possesses from the APA's description of BPD:

- Fear of abandonment*

- Unstable or changing relationships*.

- Unstable self-image, including struggles with a sense of self and identity*.

- Stress-related paranoia*

- Anger regulation problems, including frequent loss of temper or physical fights*.

- Consistent and constant feelings of sadness or worthlessness*

- Self-injury, suicidal ideation, or suicidal behavior

- Frequent mood swings*

- Impulsive behaviors such as unsafe sex, reckless driving, binge eating*, substance abuse, or excessive spending.

It is my informed opinion that if Janice and I were to gain access to Karen and Travis' home, she would be exposed as the person with all the characteristics of a person with a full-blown BPD, and she would be unable to ignore or deny it. Her fragile ego could not allow this, nor could it withstand the unmasking of the bizarre lifestyle she alone had created and maintained for too many years. We would witness the hoarding, the evidence of her chaotic home that poor Pat was subjected to.

The unflagging rage remains in Janice and me every time we think or talk of Karen. However, she unwittingly gave me a gift of enlightenment that will last a lifetime: I am certain that she is one of the worst and most injurious cases of borderline personality disorder that I have ever known.

My rage emanates from all the pummeling she gave Pat over the years they were involved. She pummeled him to his death and joined the long line of past pummelers, but she was by far the worst because she pummeled him when he was at his weakest and had no way to escape.

Can we forgive Karen for all of her pummeling of Pat and for the pummeling of Janice and me? Yes, we can, and we must forgive her seven times seventy times. Praying that Karen has peace in her life is what we offer for our forgiveness of Karen.

Chapter 39

A Happy Ending: Pat's Day!

A Celebration of His Life

It was a beautiful day in one of the most beautiful parks in Western New York: Chestnut Ridge Park. We reserved a nice pavilion in a pretty setting that Pat would have loved. The Talty's were well represented. It was also great to see some of his friends from the trailer park, the tavern that he lived above, and friends of Pat's from years ago.

Janice put together a picture board of memories of Pat, but the wind kept blowing it down, which was frustrating. We eventually wedged it in the open hatchback, and we outfoxed the wind. A lot of smiles in the photos, and we smiled again in recalling those days and events.

Bernie, Danny, and I tried to give Pat a good sendoff, but even on his special day, I had to pummel him. What is wrong with me? What I did was recall a conversation Pat and I had about the death notice for a friend of ours. Pat was expressing his disappointment that there was nothing said about our deceased friend's life, family, jobs, accomplishments, and so forth. So, recognizing an opportunity to pummel Pat, I seized the day! "Well, Pat you have to realize he wasn't a person of consequence, so there was really nothing for them to say about him." This was a very successful pummel, and I know this because of Pat's vehement and sputtering response: "Oh, yeah, he wasn't a bigshot person of consequence, so just throw him out along the road. That's nice!!" (bitter sarcasm). So, my attempt to shift a successful but hurtful pummel into a eulogy was only mildly successful: "But, regardless, Pat, on this day, you are a person of consequence in the eyes of the people here and in the eyes of those who could not be here you stand as a person of consequence, and we will love you forever. Your life and pummeling are over, but the memories you gave us will never die. Rest in peace my brother. You deserve it.

Appendix A: The ACEs Self-Assessment:

The most important thing to remember is that the ACE score is meant as a guideline: If you experienced other types of toxic stress over months or years, then those would likely increase your risk of health consequences, depending on the positive childhood experiences you had (see below).

Prior to your 19th birthday:

1. Did a parent or other adult in the household often or very often... Swear at you, insult you, put you down, or humiliate you? or Act in a way that made you afraid that you might be physically hurt?
   No___If Yes, enter 1 ___

2. Did a parent or other adult in the household often or very often... Push, grab, slap, or throw something at you? Or ever hit you so hard that you had marks or were injured?
   No___If Yes, enter 1 ___

3. Did an adult or person at least 5 years older than you ever... Touch or fondle you, or have you touched their body in a sexual way? Or Attempt or have oral, anal, or vaginal intercourse with you?
   No___If Yes, enter 1 ___

4. Did you often or very often feel that ... No one in your family loved you or thought you were important or special? Or your family didn't look out for each other, feel close to each other, or support each other?
   No___If Yes, enter 1 ___

5. Did you often or very often feel that ... You didn't have enough to eat, had to wear dirty clothes, and had

no one to protect you? Or your parents were too drunk or high to take care of you or take you to the doctor if you needed it?

No___If Yes, enter 1 __

6. Were your parents ever separated or divorced?
No___If Yes, enter 1 __

7. Was your mother or stepmother:
Often or very often pushed, grabbed, slapped, or had something thrown at her? or Sometimes, often, or very often kicked, bitten, hit with a fist, or hit with something hard? or Ever repeatedly hit over at least a few minutes or threatened with a gun or knife?
No___If Yes, enter 1 __

8. Did you live with anyone who was a problem drinker or alcoholic or who used street drugs?
No___If Yes, enter 1 __

9. Was a household member depressed or mentally ill, or did a household member attempt
suicide?   No___If Yes, enter 1 __

10. Did a household member go to prison?   No___If Yes, enter 1 __

Total Yes answers ____ (this is your ACEs score)

Author Bio

 Peter has had duel careers all of his professional life as both a practicing occupational therapist and as a professor of occupational therapy at several universities and colleges. He is most proud of having received the Teacher of the Year Award for the School of Health Related Professions at the University at Buffalo, and the Professor of the Year at Keuka College. Within his 40 plus years in academia and clinical practice he also established a private practice employing over 30 occupational therapists serving almost 40 facilities within the eight counties of Western New York.

He has written our books ranging from a guidebook for new occupational therapists (Occupation as the Key to Change), his life story (Disparity: The Autobiography of a Man with a Hungry Heart), a fictional crime novel (The Jackals' Fall) and the present biography of his brother's tragic life (The Anatomy of a Pummeled Life).

Made in the USA
Middletown, DE
24 June 2024